DEAD INTERVIEWS

DEAD
INTERVIEWS

Living Writers Meet Dead Icons

EDITED BY
Dan Crowe

GRANTA

Granta Publications, 12 Addison Avenue, London W11 4QR

First published in Great Britain by Granta Books 2013

The copyright information on page 201 constitutes
an extension of this copyright page.

Versions of some of the pieces in this book first appeared in *Zembla*.
Please see page 201 for details.

The moral right of the authors to be identified as the authors of
their work in this volume has been asserted in accordance with the
Copyright, Designs and Patents Act 1988.

'Dream Song 5' taken from *The Dream Songs* © Estate of John Berryman
and reprinted by permission of Faber and Faber Ltd.

A CIP catalogue record for this book is available
from the British Library.

1 3 5 7 9 10 8 6 4 2

ISBN 978 1 84708 827 7

Printed and bound in Great Britain by CPI Group (UK) Ltd,
Croydon, CR0 4YY

CONTENTS

INTRODUCTION

We all talk with the dead.

Some time back I was trying to come up with an idea so irresistible, so engaging, that the busy writers I was approaching would simply drop what they were doing and write for *me*. (Writers are always busy, writing or researching their books, or reviewing other people's books, or reading at literary festivals.) This was in 2003, when I was editing *Zembla*, a literary quarterly that lasted a surprisingly long two years given its cocky and slightly odd nature.

I had borrowed the name Zembla from one of my favourite books, Vladimir Nabokov's *Pale Fire* (1962). Recognized as a twentieth-century masterpiece, it is a perfect fusion of tradition, reflection, literary playfulness and distortion. (The title is taken from a section of dialogue on thievery in Shakespeare's *Timon of Athens* – although, mysteriously, when the quote is referred to, the words 'pale fire' are left out.) In the book one Charles Kinbote (aka Charles II, Charles Xavier and Charles the Beloved) writes the foreword, commentary and index accompanying a 999-line poem, entitled 'Pale Fire', by John Shade. Kinbote conjures 'explanations' from the text, speculating as to how the recently deceased poet arrived at his meanings. He is frequently nasty about his subject and clearly overwhelmed by jealousy – in other words, hardly the ideal person to provide a critique of Shade's work.

Suddenly I was gifted my killer idea: ask living authors to interview their dead literary heroes. Several interviews from *Zembla* are reprinted here, while the rest were specially commissioned for this anthology (minus the condition that subjects needed to be literary heroes – hence our dealings with Warhol and Nixon), including an extended conversation, by Joyce Carol Oates, with the iconic American poet Robert Frost.

We all talk with the dead, whether we're daydreaming about impossible conversations or asking deceased loved ones for solace and advice. In dreams, too, many of those with whom we want to converse seem unable to, as if they are shy or too busy. I liked the idea of mixing fiction with non-fiction, with the existing history of a person's life. I didn't think my idea was *totally* original; let's just say I thought it was a good one. But I didn't understand until recently how very late I was coming to the dead-interview party. Little did I know, at the time of commissioning those first interviews, that this form of dramatic writing had been around for many centuries.

Lucian of Samosata (*c.* 125–80) was the author of *Dialogues of the Dead*, which he saw as combining philosophical discussion with the art of comedy. Many of his scenes take place in Charon's boat, on the way to the Underworld. When Lucian's dialogues were rediscovered in 1499, they were translated and imitated by humanist scholars and eventually came down to later dramatists.

The form was widely used from the mid-seventeenth century, often for political purposes. Pamphlets sometimes followed the death of a well-known political figure by imagining him on arrival in Hell, conversing with some evil predecessor.

The conceit was particularly popular in France. Bernard Le Bovier de Fontenelle (1657–1757) published his highly successful *New Dialogues of the Dead* in 1683. These include conversations between ancient and modern figures, such as Socrates and Montaigne. Nearly a century later, in England, Sir George Lyttelton gave the posthumous-interview treatment to such figures as Plato, Machiavelli, William Penn and Jonathan Swift. Dr Samuel Johnson, with rare lack of perceptiveness, dismissed his efforts as little more than an attempt 'to tell the world what the world had all his life been telling him'. Well, exactly . . .

Even outside fiction, in the land of fact, things can go from the real to the unreal. The great *New Yorker* writer James Thurber, remembering the magazine's founder and first editor, Harold Ross, on a trip in Paris, recollects him complaining about a planned church visit: "'I don't want to go to Sainte-Chapelle, I've been there before", and he added something that comes back to me now as "Stained glass is damned embarrassing."' This comment makes Ross seem rather ignorant, something Thurber was perhaps overly keen to communicate in his book *The Years with Ross*. In a memoir filled with first-hand quotes, primary sources and extracts from letters and memos, was it fair for Thurber to quote Ross talking foolishly, while admitting that the quality of his recall was questionable? Does it matter? In a later edition of

The Years with Ross, the stained-glass line is quoted in the introduction, written by another respected author, as something Ross had actually said verbatim.

So what does it mean to interview someone who is dead? We want the dead to give us information, provide revelations, tell us something they didn't know when they were alive. We want to believe that they know more than we do, can advise us, help us. Where are they? Is there a God? How scared should we be? We want to ask the dead why they did what they did. We want them to say sorry. We want to say sorry to them. Above all, I think, we want to believe it is possible to talk after we die. Indeed, we want this more than anything else: more than love and food and warmth. We need to tell stories because stories *are* love, even if it's dark and we are lost, and so we continue, regardless, blind, talking to those who may not hear us. Dead people never truly die, until we are all dead. And when is that? The dead are outside time, the time we inhabit, and this crack of light between two eternities is confounding to us.

However it happens, putting words into the mouth of someone who is no longer with us finds its way, naughtily, inevitably, into the actual 'life' of the subject. We know it is fiction and yet . . . this is the way we create *our* histories (when we lack family data), as well as history itself, which is nothing if not an erratic sequence of narratives patched together by the living and the dead.

Narrative and history are the same thing at different stages of development, and that's the danger, or attraction, with books like this: that the fiction seeps into non-fiction, infecting, playfully altering (for better, for worse) what people really said, what they did, and in so doing reflecting, just a little, how the universe wants to behave. I love that.

Dan Crowe

London, June 2013

Rick Moody

interviews

JIMI HENDRIX

RICK MOODY, *an American author, was born in 1961.*

JAMES MARSHALL HENDRIX, *widely considered to be the greatest electric guitarist of all time, died in 1970.*

Will Paul Allen never stop? According to rumor and innuendo, the Microsoft co-founder and venture capitalist's most recent music-related endeavor is the financing of a public kiosk on the streets of Seattle where one will be able to speak with the deceased guitarist James Marshall Hendrix. Sources indicate that the technology is a more complex version of the A.L.I.C.E. artificial intelligence chatbot experiments, whereby powerful mainframe computers are bombarded with enough sample queries that, over time, the array of scripted replies begins to resemble a human intelligence. All extant Hendrix interviews were fed into a mainframe, during beta testing, after which programmers interrogated the Hendrix machine for months, attempting to get it to repudiate the *Band of Gypsys* period. Throughout, according to unnamed sources, the attempt was to put fans in touch with the *dead* Hendrix, who is likely to be more reflective, more nostalgic, more elegiac. Programmers have apparently achieved a remarkable and unsought result, however, in that the simulated Hendrix has begun, in considerable detail, to describe his post-mortal environment. This has led naturally to the belief among hardcore

Hendrix devotees that the Hendrix chatbot is *not* a facsimile at all, but is, rather, a genuine spirit from the afterlife. I was one of the first writers to talk with the revivified guitarist, via e-mail, about the controversy.

RICK MOODY: Given the situation in which I find myself interviewing you here, I'd like first to ask a question that Allen Ginsberg, in a dream, asked William Burroughs's wife Joan several years after her demise: 'Do the dead have memory, still love their mortal acquaintances and do they still remember us?'

JIMI HENDRIX: A cat up here has lots of time to consider, to ponder larger questions. We mean in a philosophical way. A cat has all the time in the world, because a cat does not observe the constraints of time. Dig: beliefs that adhere to your theory of relativity, space-time being curved, clumping, superstring theories, all true. Where we are, we see time like clumps of turned milk in the bottom of a glass bottle. We can look back from here, we can see people, old friends, like we see Mitch Mitchell, we see Eric Clapton, never had a very good conversation with that cat at all, and we can imagine conversations we might have had with these persons. We are hip to possible world theory, because we are high on space, we are empyreans, possibilities inherent, high on celestial bodies stretched out before us, expanses of light and nothingness. Those other conversations with Eric, they're all stretched out like beads on a strand, because it's a thirteen-dimension or fourteen-dimension afterlife, see, and all the conversations that did take place with Clapton, all the jamming, if we wasn't always trying just to play *better* than that cat, well, we could see and hear all those things too, we just choose not to.

RM: So you're saying that after death we really do land in some place where we look down on the lives of others and –

JH: Not like a floating cloud. If it was a floating cloud, we would tell you that it was a floating cloud, because we would have written some kind of thing on the subject, about floating clouds, because floating clouds sounds like some of my lyrics. But ain't no floating cloud, because there was no premonition. Ain't no white gentleman with a beard, neither.

RM: You aren't in a Judeo-Christian heavenly realm?

JH: Do they have Stratocasters where we are? That's a question for you. Do they have the cream-colored Stratocaster here? Do they have the sunburst Telecaster? Do they have the Flying V with the custom pickups, and is it easy for a cat to get replacement strings? Can we get a soft case for the guitar, for all our travel needs? One big regret is that this person, formerly called Jimi, might never have lived during the auto-tuner, which means, dig, that this person has to go onstage and tune his beloved, and it's feeding back constantly, and this person might have to struggle to tune his guitar, and this is why that person, formerly called Jimi, sometimes had to drive the guitar through the front of the amplifier, or maybe this person ain't got no choice but to stick the neck of the guitar up into the ceiling, out of frustration, because this person has feelings about what is to come, namely untimely death, dig, and this person, looking back from a place where all possible outcomes are visible, this person can see his untimely end, again and again, in different ways. So there's a frustration about the things left undone, and this person can recognize that he is coming to a place where he ain't gonna have no guitars, but where every kind of gesture that he makes will be registered in a celestial harmonic series, as guitar feedback, and maybe this is just his part of the neighborhood, who really knows. Can't play no Stratocaster, if that's what you're asking.

RM: When Miles Davis observed in his autobiography that he believed you were, at the time of your death, interested in making 'fusion' recordings, and, further, that you only recorded with the white musicians of the Jimi Hendrix Experience because you thought this was what was expected of you by a mass audience, was he correct in his judgment?

JH: Try to get Miles to turn off the damn television set and rap about this kind of thing now! You got to recognize: we had run the course, we had cleared the table, we had emptied the reservoir. And we was beginning to suffer. Man, we was suffering acutely, because, well, ordinarily we wouldn't talk about things of this nature, but since we are speaking from far beyond, from where we are empyrean, we will go ahead and say it: my mother died when I was just a young thing. She was a sweet bird couldn't do nothing but harm to herself. Then I was moving around with my dad, relocating, starting new schools, and I was taken in by my aunt, not my aunt, if you dig. That's a tale of suffering too. Wasn't till I got up here that I saw how much suffering I had gone through, saw my position in the business of music, people taking advantage, people carting away the money. I saw that people was with-holding rights to my songs. All those audiences just wanted me to play the hits over and over, do the solo just like it was on the record, which I made up on the spot the day of the recording. Only way to look back is to look at it as a time of suffering. A cat plays the trumpet and he wants to jam with me, because he admires what we're doing, and this cat went to Julliard and he's the greatest trumpeter ever in history, maybe even eclipsing Louis Armstrong, who the fuck am I to contradict this cat? I didn't finish any high school. I just played my guitar, no matter what. I found my bit of grace in this world that way. When I was playing.

RM: Can you speak a little bit more about your blackness, about your being an African-American icon in a white idiom? I know, for example, that you were turned out of a lot of hotels on your early tours, and that a cadre of rednecks attempted to keep you from playing 'The Star-Spangled Banner' in the South . . .

JH: Wasn't a color, was all possible colors. My music was an expression of all colors. Sometimes I hear the harmonic series, then I know that these things are colors. Many great com-posers past, gentlemen who I have met personally, Coltrane, Mingus, these great composers felt the torment of music and color in the way these wrestled with each other and tried to get expressed in this language of music, which is a beautiful thing, an abstract thing, a language unlike any other language. I don't know nothing about any notes on a stave, sharps and flats, but I know that up here, colors are a heartbreak and a delight. You think Martin and Malcolm just playing table tennis or some shit? They shedding tears. You think Eldridge Cleaver is not shedding tears? You think Haile Selassie is not shedding no tears? Haile Selassie is so flooded out, the cat got to pump his basement, people floating around and backstroking in his tears, and all of this is about color? Do I know that I am a black man? Was I a black man when I was dancing across the stage in outrageous fabrics? I know now, and I knew then. Do I remember that I heard the language of the Cherokee people as a little boy? Calling to me? I remember. So I took that suffering, testimonies of Lightnin' Hopkins and Muddy Waters, I made these into the music the younger people could play along with, people who were not less than those players, they just played differently.

RM: What does that imply for playing before primarily white audiences?

JH: Let me discourse on infinities. You got your set of all possible odd numbers, and that is an infinite set, am I right? Then you got your set of all possible positive and negative integers, that is also infinite, but is it not a larger set than the other we have described? Bet your white ass. Suffering of the white man is an infinite suffering, but it is a smaller infinite suffering than the suffering of the black man and the Native American man. The difference between the two is the amount that the white dudes *inflicted* on the black dudes. Audiences were going to *learn* to dig what I am saying to you. They got part the way there, until my mission got cut short.

RM: At one point, you were kidnapped by Mafia thugs, apparently on account of the shady business practices of your manager. Can you describe the experience?

JH: We were meant to play a tour that we was too exhausted to play, and we was too exhausted because we would go out every night to play with people in clubs, you know, sit in. Then when we chaperoning the women, many women, and we'd whisper the language of love into the ears of these women, and these women would inevitably succumb, and this was a thing that we needed to feel, because everywhere was deprivation, and what is the tonic that cures deprivation but the tonic of sweet love? Must have told thirty women, maybe more, that I wrote 'The Wind Cries Mary' just for them. Thing is, we were exhausted and we needed a break and things was getting worse and worse, and maybe it was a blessing in disguise, when I was jumped by these dudes, except that the gag was tight, dig, and they duct-taped our wrists and blindfolded us, and they took us to a warehouse in Brooklyn, and there they kept us for three days. I made them get me tea, for my throat, because I didn't want to catch no germ or virus locked in a warehouse. Even though I was resting up, doing nothing, I still had to play shows when I got out of there, and that means that there was just more exhaustion, see, not less. Beginning of the end right there.

RM: The kiosk where you are likely to be situated is in downtown Seattle, near one of the freeway exits, an intersection noted for its unremitting traffic snarls. Since you wrote 'Crosstown Traffic', a song that uses criticism of municipal traffic as a metaphor for romantic difficulties, I'm wondering if you could comment on Seattle's increasingly problematic gridlock situation.

JH: We were thinking back in the day that we needed to be everywhere at once. We were always thinking that since we came from nothing, since we had no money, practically no clothes, not enough food, we were thinking that we had to be everywhere and be everything to everyone, and from up here, in the empyrean, we realize that none of these things is actually true, though the motives were, well, noble and whatnot. We look down on the traffic, and we see traffic everywhere, we see the traffic in London, and we see the traffic in Rome, and we think that all the people should get out of their damn cars, and they should pound on the window of the car next to them, and they should beseech the other drivers of these cars to roll down their windows, and then they should attempt to plant kisses on the lips of the drivers of these cars, no matter whether they will be getting into a man on man type of kissing situation, no matter whether they will be kissing the proverbial fat lady. All of you all fat ladies now, down on earth. Just kiss the person in the car, tell them that they blink and are gone from this world.

Let's use your bodies while you have them, leave all your cars behind, parked on the freeway.

RM: Listening to any contemporary music these days?

JH: Little bug buzzing in your ear is music, elevator cables and counterweights going up and down is music, trucks passing on the freeway is music, dudes yammering on the television about some other war you all got yourselves into, music, sound of gunfire, over the rooftops at dawn, that's music, baby crying, being comforted by its mother, that's music, all of that is music. You don't got to listen to no shit, you don't got to listen to any Britney Spears, man, some Swedish guy with an actuarial table he got from some insurance company going to tell him how many beats he supposed to have per second, and the entire thing is played by a machine, man, that's not music.

Cynthia Ozick

interviews

HENRY JAMES

CYNTHIA OZICK, *an American short-story writer,*
novelist and essayist, was born in 1928.

HENRY JAMES, *one of the key figures of nineteenth-*
century American literary realism, died in 1916.

The interview took place at Lamb House, Rye, Sussex – rather, its precise duplicate in the Other World. The house, red brick with numerous mullioned windows, fronts the street. One approaches it along the curve of a narrow flagstoned path. Four shallow steps lead up to a white door overhung by a cornice. The modest brass knocker is tapped, and a young man responds. He is Burgess Noakes, James's valet.

HENRY JAMES (*within*): Noakes? Is it our appointed visit?
BURGESS NOAKES: Yes, sir. It's the American lady from that magazine.
HJ (*coming forward with a certain fussy anxiety*): A lady? I was rather
expecting a gentleman. Forgive me, dear madam, do come in.
– Noakes, the tea things, if you please. – Ah, my most admir-
able typewriter is just departing. Quite a morning's toil, Miss
Bosanquet, was it not? We are getting on, we are getting on!

Miss Theodora Bosanquet, James's typist (writer's cramp has in recent years
forced him to dictate), emerges from a room behind, pinning on her hat.

21

She neatly rounds James's bicycle, precariously lodged against an umbrella stand in the central hall. She nods, smiles tiredly and makes her way out with practiced efficiency.

HJ (*seating himself before a finely tiled fireplace and motioning for the visitor to join him there*): I must again beg your pardon. I discover myself increasingly perplexed by the ever-accelerating extrusions of advanced women—

CYNTHIA OZICK (*interrupting*): You don't like us. You were opinionated enough about that in *The Bostonians.*

HJ (*taken aback by this feminist brashness and glad to have Noakes deflect it with the arrival of a tray holding teacups and a variety of jellied pastries*): Thank you, Noakes. The advent of cakes, the temptation to the sweet tooth, how it brings to the fore one's recent torments at the dentist's! One must perforce disclose one's most private crannies to this oral Torquemada – which I take to be the unhappy emblem of an age of interlocutory exposure. The ladies swim in it! Especially the American ladies.

CO: I suppose that's what you were getting at in your portrait of Henrietta Stackpole, the peppy American journalist in *The Portrait of a Lady*.

HJ: May I say, *mutatis mutandis*, that *she* might have been getting at me! In point of fact, dear madam, I have in mind rather my unfortunate engagement with your predecessor, an American lady journalist representing the *New York Herald*, with whom I sat, as it were, for an interview during my American journey in 1904, my maiden voyage, so to speak, into a venture of this kind. This lady's forwardness, her hagiographical incessancy, was, in fine, redoubtable. She hastened to remark upon how I had so far, and so long, escaped the ministrations of uncanny inquirers such as herself, and undertook to portray my shrinking from her certainties as a species of diffident bewilderment. She declaimed it her right, as a free citizen of my native land, to put to me all manner of intimacies. I warned her, as I now warn you, madam, that one's craft, one's art, is in one's expression, not one's person. After you have heard Adelina Patti sing, why should you care to hear the small private voice of the woman?

CO: I gather that you intend to inhibit my line of questioning.

HJ: Madam, I do not inhibit. I merely decline to exhibit.

CO: Is that why you've had the habit of burning things? When your ailing sister Alice died, her companion, Katherine Loring, had copies of Alice's diary printed up especially for you and your brother William. You burned your copy.

HJ: Ah, the mask and armor of her fortitude, poor invalid! – and with such ironic amusement and interest in the presentation of it all. It would not, could not, do. My fraternally intimated morsels of London gossip, for the simple change and relief and diversion of it, came ultimately, and distressingly, to animate her pen. The wit of those lucubrations loomed, may I say, as a vulgar peril. So many names, personalities, hearsays, through *me*! I hardly wished to be seen as privately depreciating those to whom I was publicly civil.

CO: Yet in 1909 you might have been seen as doing exactly that. You made a bonfire in your garden of the thousands of letters sent to you by your devoted correspondents, many of them your distinguished friends. And six years later, you threw still more papers into the fire: it took you a week to get the job done. Will you agree that you've been singularly merciless to your biographers?

HJ: Put it that the forewarned victim subverts the future's cunning. I have been easier in my mind ever since, and my little conflagrations scarcely appear to have impeded posterity's massive interventions.

CO: Well, true, they haven't stopped us from speculating that you're gay and always have been.

HJ: Indeed, there has been a frequency of jolly corners . . . delightful hours with Turgenev in Paris . . . the soliloquizing intimacy of one's London hearth in winter, or the socially convenient pleasures of the ever so felicitous Reform Club . . . going in to dinner with a gracious lady on one's arm in some grand country house . . . all rewardingly gay at times, to be sure; but neither have I been spared sojourns upon the bench of desolation. Despair, I own, dogged me in particular in the year 1895, when at the opening of my play *Guy Domville*—

CO (*breaking in hurriedly*): I mean you've loved men.

HJ: And so I have. To choose but one, my fondness for the dear Jonathan Sturges, that crippled little demon, resonates unchecked for me even now. How I embraced the precious months he came to stay at Lamb House, with his mordant tongue and bright eyes, full of unprejudiced talk and intelligence. Body-blighted Brother Jonathan! Yet he made his way in London in wondrous fashion.

CO: I'm afraid we're not entirely on the same page.

HJ: The same page? Would that be an Americanism? With all your foreign influx, we shall not know our English tongue for the sacred purity it once resplendently gave out. A young American cousin, on a visit here, persisted in pronouncing 'jewel' as 'jool', 'vowel' as 'vowl', and was driven at last to deem my corrections cruel. "*Cru-el*", Rosina, not "*crool*",' I necessarily admonished. The young ladies of Bryn Mawr College, in the vicinity of Philadelphia, when I lectured there in 1905, had similar American afflictions. They would articulate the reticent 'r' in words such as *motherrrr, fatherrrr, millerrr*—

CO: I admit to that 'r' myself. But to come back to your, um, fondness for men. One of your more reckless biographers believes that in the spring of 1865, in your own shuttered bedroom in Cambridge – that's Cambridge, Massachusetts – you had your earliest experience, your *initiation première*, as you called it in your journal.

HJ: Ah, the epoch-making weeks of that memorable spring! The bliss of *l'initiation première*, the divine, the unique! It was in that very March that my first published story appeared in the *Atlantic Monthly*.

CO: We're definitely not on the same page. He claims that this *initiation première* of yours was in the arms of the young Oliver Wendell Holmes, Junior, the future chief justice of the United

States Supreme Court. He says that you slept with Holmes. Carnally.

HJ (*recoiling, and pressing his fingers to his temples, as if a familiar migraine is coming on*): My dear lady—

CO (*digging into her tote bag and pulling out a thick biographical volume*): And what about Hugh Walpole? No one burned *your* letters, after all. Here's what you wrote to your 'dear, dear Hugh': 'See therefore, how we're at one, and believe in the comfort I take in you. It goes very deep – deep, deep, deep: so infinitely do you touch and move me, dear Hugh.' Such obvious ardor! What do you say to it?

HJ: I say I deeply, deeply, infinitely favor the universalization of epistolary arson. The twaddle of mere graciousness has perhaps too often Niagara'd from the extravagances of my inkpot.

CO: And how about your 'exquisite relation' with Jocelyn Persse? A good-looking Anglo-Irishman, the nephew of Lady Gregory, thirty when you met him, you were sixty. Now it was 'my dear, dear Jocelyn'. You went so far as to ask for his photo to moon over. And then there was Hendrick Andersen, that big handsome blond Norwegian sculptor – 'I have *missed* you,' you confided, 'out of all proportion to the three meager little days that we had together. I hold you close, I feel, my dear boy, my arms around you, I draw you close, I hold you long.' So why shouldn't the homoerotic question come up?

HJ (*reddening*): Andersen's sculptures, those monstrously huge swollen ugly things. Let us pass over this unseemly subject.

CO: Here in the twenty-first century we pass over nothing, we let it all hang out. You mentioned earlier your despondency over your theatrical failure.

HJ: Madam, you hurl me from unseemliness to unseemliness! The *sacro terrore* of it all! My charmingly contemplated eloquences were vigorously upon the boards when out of nervousness I slipped out to sample a neighboring drama – *An Ideal Husband*, Oscar Wilde's juvenile folly, flailing its silly jocularity. When I returned to the St James, the last act was just finishing – there were cries of 'Author, author' – and then the hoots and jeers and catcalls of the roughs began – roars – a cage of beasts at some infernal zoo—

CO: You fell into a long depression after that. One of the many times in your life, despite brilliant friendships, fame, the richness of travel, Paris, Rome, Florence, Venice, family visits to America—

HJ: Never say you know the last word about any human heart.

CO: But George Bernard Shaw was in the audience as a reviewer that night, and he praised and championed you. You've had scores of champions and admirers – Edith Wharton, for one.

HJ: The Firebird! Her motoring habits and intentions, so potent and explicit, bent on catching me up in her irresistible talons, the whir and wind of those great pinions cold on my foredoomed brow! Oh, one's opulent friends – they cost the eyes out of one's head. Edith, always able and interesting, yet insistent and unpredictable. Her powers of devastation were ineffable.

CO: She came with her car and her chauffeur and took you away from your work. But she also facilitated it. There was that scheme she cooked up, getting your mutual publisher to give you a portion of her bestseller royalties – 8,000 dollars – while pretending they were your earnings. It was arranged so shrewdly that you swallowed it whole. And then she took up a collection for your seventieth birthday—

HJ: A more reckless and indiscreet undertaking, with no ghost of a preliminary leave asked, no hint of a sounding taken – I am still rubbing my eyes for incredulity. I undertook instant prohibitive action. It was shame heaped on shame, following as it did on the failure of my jubilant yet woebegone New York Edition, for which I had had such vain hopes, the hopes, alas, of my vanity – my labors uniformly collected, judiciously introduced by the author and improved upon according to the author's maturer lights. I have been remarkably unwanted and unread.

CO: Not lately. They make films of your stories and novels. They make novels of your life. You're an industry in the graduate schools. But isn't there something of this frustration in 'The Next Time', your tragicomical short story about a literary genius who hopes to turn himself into a hack so as to sell, to be read?

HJ (*gloomily*): With each new striving he can draw out only what lies in him to do – another masterwork doomed to obscurity. Poor fellow, he falls short of falling short!

CO: Which is more or less what happened to you when you were writing Paris letters for the *New York Tribune* for twenty dollars apiece. It ended with your getting sacked for being too good. Your brother saw it coming – he'd warned you not to lose hold of the pulse of the American public. You were over their heads.

HJ (*with some bitterness*): William instructed me, in point of fact, and not for the first time, to pander. I gave it my best, which is to say my worst. It was the poorest I could do, especially for the money! – Madam, is there to be more of this extraordinary discourse?

CO: Well, I did want to ask about the women in your life. Your tubercular young cousin, Minny Temple, for instance, who inspired your heroines Daisy Miller and Isabel Archer and Milly Theale . . . she pleaded with you to let her join you in Rome, a city she longed to see, hoping the warmer climate would cure her—

HJ: The sublime, the generous, the always vivid Minny! Yet in pursuit of my then burgeoning art, I could not possibly have taken on the care of a dying young woman.

CO: And what of your friendship with Constance Fenimore Woolson? A novelist of sensibility herself, who hung on your every word . . . you stashed her away, you kept your frequent visits to her a great secret from your London circle—

HJ: I had a dread of being, shall we say, 'linked' with Miss Woolson. I feared the public charge of an 'attachment'. But she was deranged, poor lady. She was not, she was never, wholly sane.

CO: You decided this only after she jumped out of a window in Venice and killed herself. Until then you regarded her, in your own words, as 'a deep resource'. She put aside her own work for the sake of yours. You exploited her.

James is silent. The fire's flicker darts across the vast bald dome of his Roman head. Then, with a faint groan – he is notably corpulent – he rises from his armchair.

HJ (*calling out*): Noakes, will you be good enough to escort our visitor to the door? – Ah, my dear lady, let us bring this fruitless exchange to the termination it has long merited. I observe with regret that you possess the modern manner – you proceed rather in the spirit of an assizes, you pry into the dignified celibacy of a contented bachelorhood. Heartlessly you charge on, seizing upon one's humiliations, one's defeats – Mount Ossa on Mount Pelion! You come, in fine, not to praise Caesar, but to bury him. Put it, then, madam, that you and I are not, cannot, shall never be, on the same page!

BN (*considerately*): Mind the Master's bicycle don't strike you in the shins, ma'am. Miss Bosanquet, hers was black and blue, but she's got used to it and goes round.

The interviewer picks up her tote bag (unbeknownst to James, a tape recorder is hidden in it), and also one of the jellied pastries, and wordlessly departs.

Douglas Coupland

interviews

ANDY WARHOL

DOUGLAS COUPLAND, *a Canadian writer, was born in 1961.*

ANDY WARHOL, *a leading figure in the pop art movement, died in 1987.*

Click . . . tape recorder turns on.

DOUGLAS COUPLAND: Hello, Andy.

ANDY WARHOL: Oh, hi, Doug.

DC: So then, Andy, what's the afterworld like?

AW: Ummm . . . it's not very exclusive. I mean, anybody can get in here. I'm trying to find Steve Rubell so he can set up some bouncers. Steve always had the best bouncers.

DC: Is it anything like Bloomingdale's?

AW: No, but they've got a Duane Reade here that sells concealer that flatters in my skin tone . . . I spend a lot of time there. When your skin looks good you don't have to worry about how the flash is going to make your skin look. No one wants to look dead. You need all the help you can get, even up here.

DC: What did you think of your funeral make-up?

AW: It could have been a lot more glamorous. Nobody even mentioned it anywhere in the press afterwards. My one chance for memorable make-up and they sort of blew it. But I liked the music, and Richard Gere was there and he was really cute. Is he still getting work?

DC: I just looked him up and he seems to be doing one movie a year. Nothing too memorable.

AW: Wait – what do you mean you just looked it up? Are you in a library or something?

DC: No. I'm at home. They have this thing called Google now that . . .

AW: Doodle?

DC: No. Google. It's a weird name, but you get used to it faster than you'd think. You can pretty much have the answer to anything you want now, instantly.

AW: What's *that* like?

DC: Kind of boring, actually. You'd think it'd be great, but the one thing it does is pinpoint our inability to ask good questions.

AW: Is there a Mr Google? Is he rich?

DC: Two of them. Insanely rich.

AW: You should get him to buy one of my paintings. I'll get you a commission.

DC: Oh! Oh! I can't wait to tell you . . .

AW: Tell me what? What?

DC: Your prices.

AW (*suspicious pause*): What about them? Are they going up?

DC: You'll die when I tell you . . .

AW: Too late for that. What about my prices?

DC: Guess what Christie's got for *Green Car Crash*.

AW: You mean *Burning Car*? How much?

DC: Seventy-one point seven million dollars.

Silence.

DC: Andy?

AW: Wait – is there a recession or something? Is money not worth anything any more?

DC: No. Seventy-one point seven is worth the same now as in the 80s.

AW: Huh.

DC: What's wrong?

AW: I'm really mad.

DC: Really? I thought you'd be happy.

AW: I only ever got peanuts for my stuff when I was alive. I could have had a billion dollars if I'd stuck around a bit longer.

DC: Would have, could have, should have. Nothing to be done, so best to move on.

AW: What about Jasper? What does his stuff go for?

DC: Less than yours.

AW: Really?

DC: Actually, you're absolutely king of the art world now. That foundation thing you set up really worked.

AW: My brain can't handle all these high numbers. It's too abstract. Let's talk about something else. Who's the big movie star now?

DC: Um . . . I guess Leonardo DiCaprio . . .

AW: Is he Italian?

DC: No. He's American.

AW: He should change his name to something easier to remember. Leo Casper. Is he cute?

DC: I guess so.

AW: Come on. More stars.

DC: Well, I could tell you, but they'd just be names. It's only fun when you have pictures, preferably unflattering ones.

AW: Nobody dies any more. Why did medicine wait until I died to suddenly become good? And you'd think I get gossip all the time here, but no. Michael Jackson showed up a while back, but all he does is hum snatches of his own music. He's lost in his own world. Farrah showed up ... she looked great, but I can't believe she hung on to Ryan O'Neal as long as she did. He's such a boozehound, and those Irish guys go to seed so quickly. Even in the 80s his skin was starting to look like a catcher's mitt. Liz Taylor showed up last year, too, but she has her own cloud and nobody's allowed on it.

DC: Cosmetic surgery's come a long way since 1987.

AW: Unless they can make me look like Troy Donahue, I'm not interested.

DC: Not quite. But they can make parts of your face stay totally smooth and wrinkle-free. And they inject stuff into lips now to make them look plumper.

AW: One of the benefits of trying to look like you don't care is that it keeps your skin smooth. That's why I always look the same in my photos. Who do I know who looks like they've had the most work done?

DC: That's easy. Kenny Rogers.

AW: Seriously? The country guy?

DC: He looks like his own gay twin, and slightly ... sort of ... repeat-sex-offender-ish. And Al Pacino had his eyes done and it took two decades for him to stop looking like Woody Woodpecker.

AW: Guys should never get their eyes done. It never looks good.

DC: Agreed. Oh – everyone has white teeth now. I mean *everyone*.

AW: So I bet people only remember the people with bad teeth.

DC: That's so true. Even David Bowie has good teeth now. You know, he played you in a movie.

AW: I'm not surprised. He was always watching me. It was always weird being in a room with him. Was the movie a hit?

DC: It got great reviews.

AW: So it wasn't a hit. I tried having a hit, but I never did. I mean, *all* those movies I made and the Hollywood people thought they stunk and, I mean, they weren't cheap to make, either. They cost money.

DC: Everyone makes movies these days.

AW: Really? You're kidding me. How? What are you talking about?

DC: The price of cameras and editing is almost zero. Chimpanzees can make a movie. And you can go watch them on YouTube and ...

AW: Wait ... *YouTube*?

DC: It's like Google's younger brother. It's every movie ever made whenever you want. Every TV commercial. Every everything.

AW: But wait ... is it boring in the end like Google is?

DC: Yes and no. You start out watching an old TV episode, and then you're suddenly watching puppies and kittens romping across floors, and then suddenly there's fist-fucking. It can get very random very quickly. And you can't be*lieve* the amount of porn people watch these days.

AW: Tell me something else surprising about right now.

DC: There's a black president.

AW: Seriously?

DC: Two terms, no less.

AW: Wow. And is he cute?

DC: He's very young-looking. And he skateboards.

AW: You're making this up.

DC: No, I'm not.

AW: You see? People want youth. Young, young, young. There's a part of me that's relieved I only made it to fifty-eight. It was a lot of work trying to look like I was with it. And I was feeling like a cartoon character with the wigs all the time. I mean . . .

DC: At Halloween the costume stores all have 'artist' costumes, which is basically a black turtleneck and an Andy wig.

AW: Do they pay a royalty or licensing fee for it?

DC: I doubt it. They're all made in China. Everything's made in China now. The US shipped all its jobs to China, and so now nobody has anything to do except sit around visiting Google and YouTube. I don't know if it's depressing or not.

AW: Well, at least people have something to do. And if they're inside watching movies and stuff, then they're not outside wrecking things. I always thought TV was the best babysitter of all.

DC: You have a point. Oh, there's this thing called eBay now . . .

AW (*weary sigh*): Okay, I'm listening. What is eBay?

DC: It's like the Google of shopping. You can quickly and easily go shopping for anything that's ever existed – new or old – and a few days later it's at your house.

AW: I'm jealous.

DC: And you can wipe out a collecting category in a few minutes. Like cookie jars shaped like Aunt Jemima. Or piggybanks shaped like Mr Peanut. By the way, your cookie jars went for astronomical prices at your estate sale. And they've kept their value.

AW: I was always good at finding things that were undervalued. It was like a magic trick I could do. I could pick up an object and say, 'This is really beautiful.' And then it really *would* become beautiful. I mean, Brillo boxes? Come on. But they became beautiful.

DC: Do you take pictures up there?

AW: I do. But because it's up here, everyone looks good in photos. Even me. It's not fair. There need to be a few dogs lying around to make the good shots look better. Or else it's not fun.

DC: Do you have a body up there?

AW: I do. And it's my body before I got shot, so I don't have those horrible scars any more. And not only that, but Natalie Wood recommended a really great personal trainer, so I have abs now. It's great. People who wouldn't look at me twice stop to look at my abs. I guess it's like tits on women.

DC: Do you have wings?

AW: We all do, but it's weird because people stop caring about them after a while and they let them get all ruffled and sloppy – the wings equivalent of wearing sweats to the shopping mall. I mean, if you've got something going for you, you should work it.

DC: Is there fame up there?

AW: Yes and no. Because there's no doorman, it's like we're all invited to the same party, so what's the fun in that? You bump into someone who's tasting the artichoke dip at the same time as you, but instead of it being Jackie O. or Frank Sinatra, it's some guy who drove a bus in Romania. Or some kid who carried a water bucket around their village in Africa. Everyone's polite enough, but it's kind of boring.

DC: You really nailed it with your fifteen minutes of fame quote. It's practically on the one-dollar bill now.

AW: Nobody ever quotes that right! And I've heard so many variations on it that I forget what I said in the first place.

DC: YouTube and Google are actually where everyone ends up getting their fifteen minutes of fame.

AW: This is getting too abstract for me. I know: Is Brooke Shields still beautiful?

DC: She is.

AW: Jodie Foster? She's such a smart cookie.

DC: She's still a big star.

AW: Who's turned into a disaster?

DC: Andy!

AW: Come on. They'll probably be here soon enough anyway.

DC: Let me think. Ummm ... Mickey Rourke kind of flip-flops between disaster and genius.

AW: He was that cute little kid in *Diner*. And I think he was at a lunch once ... he came with Catherine Guinness. Who else?

DC: You'll be happy to hear Liza's doing better than ever.

AW: But is she fat?

DC: Andy!

AW: Well ...?

DC: She yo-yos. She was truly massive once, but she got it under control.

AW: That mother of hers – boy, she was nuts. Halston still hangs around with her, but she's too much work for me.

Doorbell rings in the background.

DC: Andy, someone's at the door. Can you hang on a second?

AW: No way. I want to go see who just got their wings.

DC: No, wait!

AW: Oh, wow ... It's Calvin Klein. And he's looking like he's been out all night, too. I can't wait to hear where he's been.

Click ... tape recorder turns off.

Sam Leith

interviews

JOHN BERRYMAN

SAM LEITH, *a British author and journalist, was born in 1974.*

JOHN BERRYMAN, *a major figure of late-twentieth-century American poetry, died in 1972.*

The visitors' room in the locked ward has Formica tables, stacking chairs and a bare tiled floor. John Berryman comes in in striped pyjamas and a dressing gown. He looks thin. I sit across one of the tables from him, take out my tape recorder and put it on the table.

'Do you mind if I . . . ?'

'No, no.' He waves a big hand, strokes his thick beard with his knuckles, adjusts his spectacles, places the hand upside-down on the table and the elbow of his other arm in the cradle of it. He laughs. 'You need to record. This is evidence. It may need to be produced in court. Now, what is it that the *Paris Review* wants to know?'

'Granta,' I say, and he frowns, then seems not to have noticed.

'The surroundings are not –' he says, then trails off. 'Hfff . . .'

What strikes you most about Berryman, in this place, is his constant nervous motion. His head nods and wags as he talks, and his eyebrows leap and hunch. His voice comes in abrupt, sometimes explosive, fits and starts – a mumble, then an exclamation. Sometimes he seems vague; sometimes exactly emphatic. He rubs his knuckles and carves the air with his hands.

'We've been worried about you, John,' I start by saying. 'How are you?'

'I've never been better,' he says ruefully. 'I quit smoking. They have me on some sort of vegetable shakes. I do aerobics. It's awful. I'm writing, though. Plunging ahead! Plunging! I wrote a poem yesterday – or perhaps it was the day before, I don't know. Good as anything I've done. Better, even! So.'

'Can you tell me anything about your new work?'

'Well,' he says, 'they're different. I've retired Henry, and I've found a whole new metric. I've – let me read you a bit.'

He pats his pockets, then rummages in them, producing a stub of pencil and a sheet of lined notepaper, folded in four. He unfolds it, then turns it over. It's blank on both sides.

'Must have – sorry. Must be in the other one. I could have sworn. Wait – I have it by heart.' He raises himself in his seat, opens his mouth. 'You really have to get on top of these lines – they're long – and ride them down. "He –" sorry, no. "She –" That's wrong. God *damn it*. I can't . . . I can't remember a word of my new poem. It's gone. Not a word. Isn't that the damnedest thing?' He makes as if to start again, looks completely blank. 'The damnedest thing.'

'Your first master was Yeats,' I say, to get things started again. 'You ended up a long way from Yeats, though.'

'So did Yeats!' he exclaims. 'I had to get past him to go on. But the connection is there, still, underground. In the stanza, for my long poem, in the song-form . . . I met him, you know. I once saw Yeats plain. He was old and big and very gracious. Actually, I gave him a cigarette. Isn't that marvellous? They should put that on my gravestone. But there are other influences too. I loved Yeats and then I hated him and now we're on the square level. I look him in the eye. I don't mean that to sound arrogant. I think it's true.'

'You like to rank poets. Is that useful, do you think?'

'Of course!' he says. 'Poetry is competitive. You need to know who's good, and even when you won't – you know, a lot of the competition so to speak are good friends of mine – even when you won't say it you're thinking it. When I called my book *Love & Fame* I wasn't kidding!'

'What did fame do for you?'

'Ha! There, you have me. It put me frequently in the way of airports, which caused me trouble. But it gave me somewhere to speak from. I started out very sure I was underappreciated and when I *was* appreciated it freed me up. At least, to look back and see that when I thought I had been underappreciated I had actually been justly neglected. You follow me? And other things: it – fame – bought time, from teaching, writing time. Sometimes girls, though the less I say there . . .'

'You mention trouble. There's a line of yours,' I say, 'that's quoted a lot, that "the artist is extremely lucky who is presented with the worst possible ordeal which will not—"'

'"—actually kill him".' Berryman nods impatiently. 'Yes.'

'Do you still believe that?'

'I – hm – yes. Well, I was being . . . teasing. Nobody wants a tree to fall on his car. Of course, of course – what I mean is that conflict, that difficulty is where it comes from. That's how . . . in my long poem the protagonist, you know, Henry – he doesn't know what the hell is coming next. And it's usually worse than the last thing. And that – that's the action of the poem! He's heroic because he goes on, even though he doesn't always want to. He can't help it.'

'Were you afraid,' I ask, 'that if your own life became less chaotic your poems would fall off?'

'I certainly didn't go looking for trouble. That's simplistic. The suffering happens anyway. Art comes out of that, or doesn't. I've said before that I disagree very strongly with Eliot's line about impersonality – he's exactly wrong. It's personality that holds all my poems together – not my personality, you understand, but the personality of the poems. And that's made under pressure.'

His eyes, behind his big horn-rimmed glasses, are looking side-ways. There's a slight yolkiness to them. One finger is extended, to emphasize his point. He looks at his finger as if it doesn't belong to him. He seems, for a moment, to lose his thread, then finds it again.

'I don't mean that poems about loss, and grief, and fighting with God, and all that jazz – that those poems have to be solemn. I feel for Henry – but he's a jerk! I feel for him, partly, because I *made* him a jerk. So you can feel close to your character but – Henry's self-pity is funny, don't you think? I read those Songs and I laugh my ass off.'

'Mel Brooks,' I tell him, 'said, "Tragedy is when I cut my finger; comedy is when you walk into an open sewer and die."'

'Did he?' says Berryman, with less curiosity than the question mark implies.

There's a long pause. You always make a fool out of yourself when you meet your heroes. I'm flustered, but blush and move on. Because this is my first and last chance to sit in the same room with John Berryman – I want to offer him a cigarette, like he offered Yeats, but I don't have one and there's no smoking here and he's given up anyway – I tell him that I named my cat after Henry.

'That's a terrible name for a cat,' he says. He looks flattered.

I want to tell him that for many years I kept a paperback copy of *77 Dream Songs* in my computer case and that it went with me wherever I travelled and was read and reread and mattered hugely to me when I was blue, but I worry that might cross the line between journalism and stalking, so instead I say, hesitatingly, that the experience of the reader is that these Songs are friendly. If you live with them enough you feel Henry is your friend.

'I don't set myself up as a critic of my own poems,' he says. 'I'm interested in the things people say about them. I'm glad when assistant professors become associate professors by establishing that I am using a Hebrew meter or that Henry's friend is called Theophilus, or that such and such a Song is modelled on 'Easter Wings' or – heh – what have you . . . but. Sure: friendly. Personality, again, see? I gave Henry a friend – boy, did he need one – and I think he's a friend of mine – though I made him up, so it's an unequal relationship obviously.'

'Like Henry's with God?'

'I suppose you could say that. I'm not sure I would. But God is a presence. I was brought up very strong Catholic, very conventional and down the line. I adored our priest. When my father killed himself that – whoosh! – went. I was twelve. There was a falling-out. But I've always been very interested in theology. In the Songs there's a *squabble* with God: Henry's – do you remember my line?' and Berryman, nodding his head back and forth with the emphases, recites from memory: '"Henry sats in de bar & was odd,/ off in the glass from the glass,/ at odds wif de world & its god" and so on. So there's that. He's sulking, you know. God's Henry's enemy. And that sulk is mine.'

'How,' I start to ask – and here, I'm dangerously close to territory prohibited in the terms under which permission for this interview was granted – 'has your understanding of God changed?'

'I did have a conversion experience – very powerful, very sudden and entirely authentic to me – when I was in the bin the last time, to the idea of a God who wasn't just the grounds for existence but what I've called a God of *rescue*, a God who would take a personal interest in the troubles and bothers of a forked thing like you or me. That affected me profoundly.

'I wrote about that in my last book [*Love & Fame*; *Delusions, Etc.* and his unfinished novel *Recovery* were published posthumously] in the 'Addresses to the Lord', which were prayers, in a very direct style.'

'The book had a pretty mixed reception. A lot of it even your admirers thought messy and rushed.'

'That baffled me. I knew that these were goddamned good! Cal [Robert Lowell] said so too. American letters is very atheistic, of course. You'd expect resistance. But *technically* they are good. Of course I didn't expect Allen [Tate] to like those poems – I don't think he was equipped to do so – but I expected him to read them seriously.' There is a flash of anger in his voice. 'I wrote him to say – and I didn't hear back.' (This is on the record. The card Berryman sent said just, 'YOU HURT ME'; Tate wrote, 'This was my intention', and put it aside.)

'Allen was a good critic. But he turned on me, and I think that was personal. I think he was chewed up by not being the poet he wanted to be. Maybe I wasn't the poet he wanted me to be, in that book. He wasn't the critic Randall Jarrell was, or the pal. I miss having Randall around. I do so miss Randall. And Cal never visits.'

He shrugs, pulls the lapel of his dressing gown tight round him and stares at the stalled clock on the wall behind me. 'I don't mean to complain. You know, when you've lived as long as I have people fall away. You just go on, all each damned day. You can't help it. Allen probably didn't mean to hurt my feelings.'

I look at my list of questions, again – the facetious ones I had in mind to ask him, from the Songs: 'Is life a handkerchief sandwich?', 'Should Henry have come out and talked?', 'Is that thing on the front of your head what it seems to be?' They feel not playful and warm, now, but silly and small.

There's a detail I can't get past. I want to put it to him, but I don't quite know how. One eyewitness told the local paper that when he walked out on the Washington Avenue Bridge, just before he jumped, he turned and 'waved goodbye', and a biographer claimed that 'he made a gesture as if waving, but he did not look back'.

'Um, John. Is it true that you waved?'

'Waved?' he says vaguely – and looks puzzled. Then something passes behind his eyes, as if a thing he'd dreamed and then forgotten has come back to him. He looks at me, and asks sharply, 'Where am I? What is this place?'

Geoff Dyer

interviews

FRIEDRICH NIETZSCHE

GEOFF DYER, *an English writer, was born in 1958.*

FRIEDRICH NIETZSCHE, *a German philosopher, died in 1900.*

The following interview took place in Turin in May 2004. It had been arranged by the *Journal of the London Philosophical Society*, who, after listening to the tapes, decided that, even with editing, it would not be suitable for their pages. The unedited transcript is published here for the first time.

GEOFF DYER: Hello. I really appreciate your taking the time to do this interview. We'll speak for maybe half an hour. It's very informal, just a chat, really. How do you like to be addressed, by the way – would that be Herr Nietzsche? Friedrich?

FRIEDRICH NIETZSCHE: Friedrich is fine.

GD: How about Zarathustra? Ha ha . . . No, just joking. (*Sniffing*) OK, let's just check that this tape machine is working. The last time I interviewed someone it wasn't. We spoke for ages – all sorts of really great stuff. Get back home and listen to the tape and it's totally blank. Nothing. Had to make it all up afterwards. Don't want that to happen here, do we? So can we get some level? What did you have for breakfast this morning, Friedrich?

FN: I had a cappuccino and a cornetto.

GD: How was it? Not too foamy?

FN: It was very nice, thank you.

GD: And the cornetto? Do they still keep aside the nicest pastries for you?

FN (*hesitantly*): I think they might, yes.

GD: And how did you get here?

FN: I walked.

GD: Good for you. Bit of exercise. Get the old brain oxygenated. (*Sniffing*) OK, is it rolling, Bob? . . . Yep, that's great. The level's fine. We're ready. So, Herr Nietzsche, you're the author of many books which are considered to be among the most influential and controversial ever written. Maybe I could start by asking why they're still considered so controversial?

FN: When you propose the revaluation of all values—

GD: Let me put it another way. Why do you write such excellent books? Why are you so clever?

FN: I—

GD: Sorry to interrupt, but I should explain for people who don't know Herr Nietzsche's works that I was alluding to the chapter titles from his autobiography, *Ecce Homo*. The last chapter is 'Why I am a destiny'. Can you believe that? Were you, like, joking, or did you really mean that?

FN: I was being exuberant.

GD: You must've expected to get some stick for that, though, right? But then, like I said, you're no stranger to controversy. You famously said, 'God is dead.' What did you mean by that? Could you spell it out for our readers?

FN: Well, if you go back to the nineteenth century . . .

GD: Right, right. Because back then everybody believed in God. Like now, if you said God is dead, people would be, like, big fucking whoopee. Here's someone else trying to work the old Hitchens–Dawkins hustle. Unless you said Allah was dead. Then you'd get a real shit storm breaking over your head! But of course by saying God was dead you played your part in killing him off, right? Good man. Anyway, let me ask you another question. Along with Freud and Marx, you're credited with being one of the three thinkers who exerted most influence on the twentieth century. Now, Marx obviously has been made to look pretty stupid, what with the collapse of the Soviet Union and Stalin and the Gulag and everything. As for Freud, well, his stock is way down too. He's toast, practically. Which just leaves you. Congratulations! Effectively, you've won the Big Brother of enduring philosophical influence. Ha! The others have been voted out of the house. How does it feel? How does it feeeeeel? D'you like Dylan, by the way? We'll come back to him in a minute . . . Seriously, how does it feel to go from being a complete unknown for most of your life, to being the number one, the *numero uno* philosopher, the last man standing, so to speak?

FN: It feels like a vindication. But the real purpose, the real struggle, is not to overcome others, but to overcome yourself.

GD: We're talking about *The Will to Power*, right? I wanted to ask you about that, because it's probably the most controversial of all your books—

FN: It's not my book. That was put together by my sister, Elisabeth.

GD: Yeah, but it's your stuff, right? Anyway, I want to press you a bit more about some of the controversial aspects of your work. How do you respond to the charge that your writings led directly to Hitler and the Holocaust and everything?

FN: It's nonsense.

GD: Well, there's that book by John Carey, *The Intellectuals and the Masses*, where he pretty much makes that claim. And you were always glorifying war and the warrior spirit and we know Hitler was a big fan.

FN: This is too—

GD: You were great friends with Wagner, right? You considered him to be the greatest genius ever. Now, Wagner was a notorious anti-Semite, wasn't he? What about you? Are you anti-Semitic?

FN: Wagner's anti-Semitism was one of the things that—

GD: Let me ask you straight out? Do you feel at all responsible for the Second World War and the Holocaust? A straight answer: yes or no?

FN: No.

GD: Well, you would say that, wouldn't you? You're hardly going to hold up your hands and say, 'Yes, fair cop. I was responsible for the deaths of fifty million people or whatever in a crisis like no other: the greatest catastrophe ever to engulf mankind!' And it's not just you. I mean, even in Schubert, you can see some kind of proto-Führer worship in that song cycle of his, *Take Me to Your Lieder*, or whatever it's called.

FN: My sister Elisabeth—

GD: Yes, I wanted to ask you about her. She was a great friend of Hitler's – is that right?

FN: My sister was a stupid bitch!

GD: Whoa! Touched a nerve there, yes?

FN: The thing that most disturbed me about the Eternal Recurrence was the thought of meeting my sister again.

GD: Well, that was going to be my next question. This idea of the Eternal Recurrence. I've got to say, I don't really understand it . . . Do you really mean that everything that happens happens again and again?

FN: Now and throughout all eternity.

GD: Even this conversation?

FN: Yes, unfortunately.

GD: Even my saying to you, 'Even this conversation?'

FN: Yes.

GD: Even my saying to you, 'Even my saying to you, "Even this conversation?"'

FN: Yes, even that. And that joke, if you don't mind my saying, is wearing a little thin.

GD: Fair enough. Just trying to keep things relaxed. Now, I know you say you got the idea of the Eternal Recurrence 'six thousand feet beyond man and time', but what about *Groundhog Day*? Was that an influence?

FN: What is this Groundhog Day?

GD: It's a film, but I reckon you knew that anyway. And I think that when you say you had this idea six thousand feet above mankind you're maybe saying, in a kind of code, that you saw it as an in-flight movie. Any truth in that?

FN: I don't know what you are talking about.

GD: I'm not accusing you of plagiarism. There's no need to be so defensive. I'm just asking if you saw a film.

FN: No.

GD: How many times did you not see it? Did you not see it over and over again, throughout all eternity?

FN: As I said before, I really don't know what you're talking about.

GD: Well, *Groundhog Day* is this really cool movie with Bill Murray. He plays this guy who finds he just keeps repeating the same day over and over. It seems to me that that's what you're saying with the idea of the Eternal Recurrence pretty much.

FN: I've not seen that film.

GD: Well, if you haven't you should. You can rent it. And then there's some Dylan I wanted to ask you about. Bob Dylan, you've heard of him, right?

FN: I don't know his work.

GD: Well, in 'Stuck Inside of Mobile with the Memphis Blues Again' he talks about going through things twice. And in 'Queen Jane Approximately' he's sick of repetition. Do you think he's talking about the Eternal Recurrence?

FN: He could be . . .

GD: So how do you feel, personally, about the Eternal Recurrence?

FN: It is a terrible idea, a horrible idea. The ultimate test. It is only the *Übermensch* who can come to terms with the idea of the Eternal Recurrence.

GD: *Übermensch?*

FN: It has been variously translated, either as Overman or Superman—

GD: Oh, I see. It's one of those George 'the English simply will not do' Steiner words, is it?

FN: It's a vision of what we might become. As I wrote in *Zarathustra*: 'Man is a rope stretched between ape and superman.'

GD: OK, let's talk about *that* for a moment. So you're into the idea of the Superman? I find that surprising.

FN: Why? What do you mean?

GD: I mean Superman is DC, whereas most people who are hip to this kind of thing would definitely be on the side of Marvel. You know, Spider-Man, the Fantastic Four, Silver Surfer, Thor. I bet you like Thor, don't you?

FN: Why?

GD: Well, you know, you said you liked to philosophize with a hammer and Thor has his hammer.

FN: These things I do not know about . . .

GD: Well, what *about* the Thing. 'It's clobberin' time!' Effectively, that's what you were saying, wasn't it? Conventional morality was going to get a clobbering from you . . . Actually, while we're on the subject of the Fantastic Four, do you think the reason Sue Richards turned invisible was because she worried that when Reed came to see her he was bringing his whip with him – whip, in this case, being his rubbery arm? Just joking. I'm really thinking about your ideas in *Beyond Good and Evil* . . . Perhaps you're more of a super-villain than a super-hero. So let me ask you this: do you see yourself (*stifled sniggering*) as the Doctor Doom of Western philosophy?

FN: Mine is a philosophy of affirmation.

GD: So you think Schopenhauer is more like Doctor Doom? Or maybe it's Cioran: *The Trouble with Being Born*. Man, that guy makes Doctor Doom look like an optimist. Anyway, that's beside the point. Tell me, do you believe in reincarnation?

FN: I believe you are reincarnated as yourself.

GD: Let me ask you about something else. You said that the thought of suicide gets us through many a bad night. What did you mean by that?

FN: What do you mean, what did I mean by that? How much simpler can I put it?

GD: Well, maybe you could just spell it out, you know, for our readers.

FN: I mean that the thought of suicide gets you through—

GD: . . . many a bad night? We're going round in circles – it's that old Eternal Recurrence again. Ha! OK. Now let's get serious here for a moment, let's talk about Dionysus. *The Birth of Tragedy*: published in 1872 when you were, what, twenty-eight or something?

FN: That's correct.

GD: OK, so you claim that Greek tragedy wasn't just due to Apollonian restraint or grace or whatever, but to primeval forces or instincts that found uninhibited expression in the singing and dancing rituals of people who were into the cult of Dionysus. After that you left academia and became a kind of wanderer or renegade, bumming around Europe, lodging in poorly heated rooms. In one of these, near Nice, you got yourself a little stove—

FN (*warmly*): My 'fire-idol', I called it.

GD: Right. And you used to leap and prance around this fire idol. But then, in December 1889, a friend arrived here in Turin, went up to your room and was appalled to see you, quote, 'leaping and whirling around in a dance of Dionysian frenzy'. Now, you were an amazingly prophetic writer and the question I want to put to you is this: do you think that in some way the stuff you wrote about Dionysus and all this dancing around the fire, did you in some way foresee the Burning Man Festival?

FN: Again, I don't know what you are talking about.

GD: Well, let me quote some more of your own words. You know, a lot of people have this condescending attitude to Burning Man, dismissing it as a bunch of hippies taking drugs and freaking out in the desert. But you've got the answer to them – I've got the quote here: 'There are some who, from obtuseness or lack of experience, turn contemptuously or condescendingly away from such phenomena. But such poor souls have no idea how corpse-like and spectral this "healthy-mindedness" of theirs looks when the glowing life of the Dionysian revellers roars past them.'

FN: Perhaps I would like to go, to see this.

GD: Not to *see* it, dude – to *participate*! You know that line you quoted earlier: 'Man is a rope stretched between ape and superman.' I think it should be rewritten: 'Man is a rope stretched between ape and *Burning* Man.' Thus spake Zarathustra!

FN: Perhaps.

GD: Actually there's another reason why I bring up all this Burning Man stuff. There's a book I got sent recently in which the author says that you took opium, at first for headaches and quite a bit after that, basically for what would now be called recreational purposes. This book also says that you were supplied with some other substance which may have been hashish or cocaine; either way, the evidence, quote, 'points rather to a psychedelic "trip"', unquote. Any truth in that?

FN: What book is this?

GD: I've got it here in my bag, hang on ... There you go. Perfectly respectable book. Not published by, you know, Cloudy Bong Water Books in California or something, but by Yale University Press: *Zarathustra's Secret* by Joachim Köhler.

FN: He is a specialist and specialists possess the tremendous stupidity of the force of gravity – which is why people like him often achieve a great deal. There is no secret ...

GD: What? You mean, you were there but didn't inhale? Yeah, right! You don't need to believe in the Eternal Recurrence to have heard that one before.

FN: I really must insist ...

GD: Well, listen, Friedrich, off the record. When we started this interview I was more than a little buzzed myself – probably why I've been talking so much. Truth is, I was a bit nervous, meeting a famous philosopher and everything, so I felt I had to have a little pick-me-up, and I mean something a bit more potent than a double espresso. (*Sound of rustling*) And now, enlightening though our talk is, I'm actually feeling I could do with a bit more in the way of stimulation, so how about you and I have a little line of this. (*Sound of snorting*) Sure you won't partake? No? Hey, I thought you were the real bad-ass of the philosophical world. I thought you said you were dynamite. Oh, well. Waste not, want not! (*More snorting*) Now, you know that line of yours – not the line that's just gone up my nose, I mean line as in line of poetry – 'Have you ever known a moment when you would say to yourself: "You are a God and never have I heard anything more divine."' Well, Freddie boy, I think I know what you were talking about! Whooo! This shit really *is* dynamite! Now, well, where were we? Let's move on to something else. OK. We're in Turin and not far from here there's the place where you saw a taxi driver whipping his horse and you really lost it, flung your arms around the horse's neck, right? After that you went sort of nuts. (*Sniffs*) What was it about that scene that got to you?

FN: I don't wish to talk about that.

GD: Did you feel sorry for the horse?

Long pause.

GD: Did you identify with the horse?

Long pause.

GD: Have you seen that movie *The Horse Whisperer*?

Long pause.

GD: D'you like Cormac McCarthy?

Long pause.

GD: Have you heard of Red Rum?

Long pause.

GD: Oh, c'mon, why the long face? – as the barman said to the horse. (*Pause*) You've heard it before, right? OK. Well . . . Um, now, I hope you don't mind my asking but, well, let's cut to the chase. It's pretty well known that you had syphilis and that that had something to do with your going nuts . . .

FN: I don't want to discuss my private life.

GD: Fair enough, but you know . . . Let's talk about something else. What about *The Gay Science*? That must've been one of the first openly gay books ever written?

FN: I don't understand.

GD: Well, I mean, maybe you could tell me about it. Is it about the way that some people are biologically, that is to say, scientifically, determined to be gay?

FN: I don't understand.

GD: I think you do. I think you're being more than a little coy. Shall I be frank, Freddie? This cat Köhler, he claims that you picked up the pox, the syphilis which probably played a part in your having all these mental problems after the horsey episodey, was contracted – and I think you know what's coming – (*whispers*) at a gay brothel in Genoa.

FN: Nonsense.

GD: So why are you blushing?

FN: I'm not blushing.

GD: Let me ask you straight out in a kind of Paxman style: are you saying that you've never ever, not once in your life . . . sucked dick?

Pause.

FN: I shall turn my head away. Henceforth that will be my sole negation.

GD: Ah, you're trying to stonewall me. So to speak. Let's put it another way. Now, I'm no psychoanalyst, I'm not Adam Phillips or Darian fucking Leader, but if we think about that episode with the horse which you refused to speak about and now you won't talk about this either. Could that be because you are actually (*sniggers*) what is vulgarly known as a bit of a knob jockey?

FN: I am wishing to terminate this interview.

GD: Oh, c'mon, I'm just pulling your leg. Actually, speaking of pulling . . . You were banging on about this idea of self-overcoming blah blah, right? But in this book of Köhler's it says that your friend Dick Wagner wrote to your doctor that all the head- and eye-aches you suffered from were the result of, not to put too fine a point on it, excessive jerking off. So what he was saying, effectively, is that in spite of all this talk about self-overcoming you actually spent your time (*stifling laughter*) . . . coming all over yourself! (*Loud laughter*)

FN: This interview is—

GD: Sorry, I was joking. No, sorry, really, that was out of order. *Es tut mir leid.* I shouldn't have had that second line. To be honest, my head feels like it might explode. Hey, Freddie, come back. Let's talk about the Eternal Recurrence again. Christ! (*Shouting*) Sorry, I mean *anti*-Christ! Hey, hey, if you do ever get to Burning Man make sure you check out camp Jiffy Lube . . . (*More quietly*) Oh, c'mon, don't be such an uptight Prussian wanker! Shit . . . Man, I am seriously fucked up . . . Let's turn this thing off . . .

A. M. Homes

creates Tom, who interviews

RICHARD NIXON

A. M. HOMES, *an American author, was born in 1961.*

RICHARD NIXON, *the 37th president of the United States, died in 1994.*

'TOM' *lived next door to the Nixons.*

The following is an interview conducted with former president Richard Nixon at his home in New Jersey. I lived next door to the Nixons as a child and was in my first semester in college when I turned in the assignment – to interview someone 'living a political life' – for which I got a B+ from the professor. My professor 'detested' Nixon and felt the need to show me documents which he claimed proved that Nixon wilfully extended the Vietnam War in order to gain a second term.

Our meeting took place early on a Saturday morning. The former president opened the door himself, looking relaxed in a cardigan sweater over his shirt. I noticed he was wearing slippers instead of shoes.

TOM: Hello, Mr President.

RICHARD NIXON: Glad to see you. Come in, come in. You're all grown up. I remember you as the little boy next door who was always losing a ball or a Frisbee or accidentally getting something stuck on the roof.

T: That's me, sir. I really appreciate your taking the time to talk with me. I've been a fan – ever since I was a kid. And well, now that I'm studying history, I'm just filled with questions.

RN: Well, you of all people – I actually owe something to. Do you remember when our dog got off the leash and I was out there in the street trying to run after him. And I'm not much of a runner. I've had a hell of a time with my legs over the years – that's why I'm wearing these pansy slippers, to keep the pressure off my feet. But anyway, you caught the dog for me – and there would have been hell to pay in this house if the dog got away.

T: Happy to do it, sir.

Quickly I make a few mental notes, not wanting to miss anything. The setting is a powder-blue living room, pristine, lost in time, a powder-blue crushed-velvet sofa, two large comfortable chairs, some chintz pillows and a creamy white carpet – it's like sitting in an inverted sky. Photographs in silver frames cover every surface and against the wall there's a beautiful antique clock with a long pendulum quietly tick-tocking back and forth. Across the room I spot a well-stocked liquor cabinet and an old console television – which the president catches me looking at, as it seems out of place.

RN: I saw myself win on that and would you believe it still works. (*He turns it on and off with an ancient remote – each button looks like a giant tooth.*) All right, then, enough with the tour. As I long as I'm still living here it's home, not a museum. (*He pauses to clip the microphone I'm handing to him onto the edge of his sweater.*)

Before we get into it – I just want to say, the last time I did this kind of thing it ended up biting me in the ass, so it's not something I'm looking forward to. (*Adjusting the microphone*) That said, you've been helpful in the past and I suppose it's the thing to do – to repay the favor.

T: Thank you, sir, I understand. And before we start I also want to say that you and Mrs Nixon were always the best at Halloween. We always liked going to your house for trick-or-treating. You gave good candy.

RN (*laughs*): That's not a compliment I've heard before.

T: I don't know if you remember there were some years when people were worried about folks poisoning the candy or putting needles in it and my father always said, 'Go to the Nixons, you know that they're safe.'

RN: Well, it's nice to know people feel good about you. It wasn't always that way – there were years when I have no doubt a good many people would have liked to put pins in my candy.

T: Anyway, I just wanted to thank you again.

RN: All right, then. Let's get down to it.

T: I guess my first question goes back to the dog. Did you always like animals or were they really a PR stunt, as some people have suggested about Checkers?

RN: Well, of course we had Checkers, who became quite famous after my speech. I could never tell what moved people more – the line about the dog or the bit about Pat's cloth coat. And then we had an Irish setter, King Timahoe. Tricia had Pasha, a little Yorkie, and Julie had a small French poodle called Vickie. And at San Clemente we had a bunch of dogs – for a while people were always giving us dogs. It became the thing to do, give the Nixons a dog. I think the only other president who received so many animals as gifts may have been George Washington. Anyway, yes, I like dogs – it's nice to have someone around who thinks you're great no matter what.

T: Did you have pets as a child?

RN: Tom, I grew up in tough times – we were poor. Animals weren't coddled the way they are today. You didn't take them to the doctor every time they sneezed. There were animals around and maybe a chicken or two running around the yard. The Nixons were practical people.

T: Sir, I can't help but notice that we're sitting here surrounded by photos of you with various foreign leaders, with Elvis Presley, but I see some pictures that are clearly more personal – your family?

RN: This one here is my brother Harold, who was sick for a long time before he passed. My mother knocked herself out trying to nurse him back to health. I'll tell you a little secret. My mother was known for her pies, made the best damned pie you ever ate – cherry was her specialty. And when my mother took my brother Harold to Arizona for his tuberculosis, my father made the pies himself. They weren't quite the same as my mother's, but they were darned good. He wasn't ever going to quit. Nixons don't quit. One day I went off to school – I was in college at the time – and Harold said good-bye to me that morning and I never saw him again. Someone came and found me in the library and told me to get home. My brother Arthur – only lived to be seven. There was a lot of tragedy in the family – a darkness. You know I was offered free tuition at Harvard, but due to Harold's illness I was needed at home – to work in the store – and so I attended Whittier College.

T: And is that a wedding picture of you and Mrs Nixon?

RN: Yes. We met in Whittier in 1938, playing opposite each other in a community theater production of *The Dark Tower*. Pat was a high school teacher and I fell for her right away. Took me a while to convince her, though. And I was a real sport. I used to drive her on her dates with other fellas before she said yes to me. Truth is I didn't want to let her out of my sight.

T: Did Mrs Nixon enjoy public life? I remember my mother saying something about her really disliking it.

RN: Pat never liked politics, and I guess the truth is I take these things hard and that's hard on everyone. I was very surprised by the loss of the 1960 race with Kennedy. I'm still not sure wasn't fixed in some way … (*coughs*). And then in '62 I ran for governor in California and lost and I think Pat hoped that would be the end of it. In fact, I may have promised her that I'd stay out for a while. We moved to New York. And things were good, but you know, when you've got the heart and mind for politics, it's hard to stay quiet – and so when I decided to run again in 1968, she put up with me and I think she was pretty well thrilled that we won. She was such a private person, a very decent and loving wife and mother, and I think it's asking a lot of someone to be the first lady – to put up with all the things she had to put up with. That's why, every Valentine's Day, I always tried to do a good job letting her know how grateful I was.

T: Do you worry about how people see you? We live in such a confessional culture, where everyone is going to therapy and in a twelve-step program. I'm curious about what it's like for you. I mean, hell, even your psychiatrist wrote a book, *The Will to Live*. What do you think about that?

RN: I never went to a psychiatrist. (*He shifts uncomfortably on the sofa.*)

T: Dr Arnold A. Hutschnecker?

RN: Hutschnecker – well, yes, I went to him, back when he was an internist. I had a problem with pain in my back and wasn't sleeping well. Over the years we became friends. I'd call on him when I needed some advice. Sometimes there are things someone needs to try out on another fella, to get a kind of reading on. He was a good man and a very good friend.

T: He accompanied you to Mrs Nixon's funeral?

RN (*tearing up*): I asked him to come with me to Pat's funeral. I was quite broken up about her death. What a life she lived, so much she did for others.

T: Dr Hutschnecker held your hand at the funeral.

RN: Did he? Well, he was a very good friend. And for a man I guess I am sometimes quite emotional. I'm not going to be ashamed of it – I show my feelings. Now, how about asking me some real questions – not just stuff like this?

T: Can you talk a little bit about why you had your desk wired with five recording devices? What did you think you might needs the tapes for?

RN: I wasn't the first president to record conversations. Roosevelt did it and then Kennedy and LBJ – he was the one who clued in to the whole thing. And, you know, it was the time as well, a technological boom, so we were playing with these new toys.

T: Five?

RN: No, not that many.

T: Five in the desk and two in the wall.

RN: Well, whatever it was, we had those.

T: And one in the Lincoln bedroom. And your office in the Executive Office Building.

RN: You know, it was actually the Secret Service who installed and maintained that equipment.

T: At your direction.

RN: Are we going to continue along this line – because if so I'm not interested. (*Pause*) What's interesting to me is that everyone who comes in here asks the questions again and again, year after year, like they're expecting the answers to change. I'm not suddenly going to become a different person. There's not some big ah-ha moment where I'm going to be a different Richard Nixon. I'm the same guy I always was, take it or leave it. People act like they're waiting for me to apologize, to be sorry. I'm not sorry. I've got nothing to be sorry about. I was a damned good president. And yes, I can see how things got kind of convoluted and misconstrued around all that Watergate crap, but trust me, that's small potatoes when it comes to what a president has to do. If you want my honest opinion . . . I think what's happening is that the more folks come around, they realize I'm not such a bad guy compared to what's out there . . .

T: Over the years, do you feel there's been a shift in your reputation?

RN: These things take time. It takes time to build a career, a reputation. When I was in the White House I made a few bad choices. Some of it was who I surrounded myself with, the advice I got. What I thought was possible might have been going too far – maybe we did some things that we shouldn't have technically, but we did them for the right reasons. We did them for the good of the country.

T: What do you tell people who want to go into politics?

RN: It's not for the faint of heart. Know your friends and know your enemies even better.

T: You had an active enemies list?

RN: Anyone doing something interesting has enemies. There are journalists whose entire careers were made on trying to undo me. I didn't take it personally. (*Pause*) That's not correct, I did take it personally.

T: Is it true you tried to have a journalist named Jack Anderson assassinated?

RN: I haven't heard that name in a long time. Looking back, I wonder who was trying to assassinate whom. There was no love lost between Anderson and myself. As president you realize that you're not going to make everyone happy, but the point is you get the job done. Washington is a rats' nest of people out to get you, to make you look bad. I was never a media darling. I always felt like an outsider – like Pat and I just weren't like the rest of them – and in some ways that was a very good thing, because we weren't drawn into their nonsense.

T: What do you want to be known for?

RN: It's hard to know where to begin. I was enormously successful reopening relations with China – I single-handedly changed the course of history with that one. And then on my watch we also signed one of the first treaties limiting the nuclear arms race and did a hell of a lot to clean up segregation in the South. I started the Environmental Protection Agency and I balanced the national budget. Hell, I bet no one ever thinks about that, and even women, I did some pretty good things for women, even though in my personal opinion I fundamentally don't believe in women working outside of the home if it can be helped, but I recognize that my opinions might seem a little old-fashioned – my wife and daughters often reminded me of that.

T: I'm curious to know what the biggest challenges were.

RN: Sticking to your convictions even when it's not popular. The whole China idea came about when I got interested in the country in the late 1950s. As you know, I have been strongly anti-communist – my work on the House Un-American

Activities Committee made that clear – but I thought it made sense that in order to pull Russia in closer we needed to include China. Some of my toughest critics, George McGovern among them, said that I had a very practical approach to the two superpowers – that being China and the Soviet Union. I did my damnedest – and you know, son, sometimes that's just not good enough for folks. No one wanted me to go to China, but I think it's the best thing I ever did. The Chinese are very smart. It wouldn't surprise me if one day there's a Chinese-American president. Hard-working, they stop at nothing to get ahead.

T: Was Dr Kissinger helpful with China?

RN: Henry was opposed to the idea initially, but I let him know that if he didn't get on board, I'd find someone else to do it – and he got into the idea and did a hell of a job setting things up over there. I don't know if you remember, but I went back to China in 1976 at the personal invitation of Chairman Mao – that was very gratifying.

T: I guess I'm curious to know what if anything you'd like people to know about you.

RN: I want them to know that I'm a good person. That if sometimes I did the wrong things it was for the right reasons. I only wanted the best for my country and I damned near killed myself trying to get us into a good position. I meant no harm. I want people to think well of me, not to dwell on my errors – we all make mistakes – but to remember the good I did. I'm very proud of what I was able to accomplish and I'd hate for people to lose sight of all that and just dwell on these couple of negative things.

T: Do you feel like the American people know who Richard Nixon is?

RN: I'm not the kind of guy who lets it all hang out. We've become a country of people who live to tell it all – who want to go on television and spill their guts. I'm never going to be that man. I find that kind of behavior undignified. That said, I am a guy who likes to have a little fun. I was on the *Jack Paar Show*, and I did *Laugh-In*, I said, 'Sock it to me.'

T: I read somewhere that you always wanted to conduct an orchestra?

RN: I love music. I played the piano since I was a boy. And let's see, I am fond of the score from *Victory at Sea*, and also Liszt's *Préludes*. I may have told this story before, but for my second inauguration they asked what I'd like the orchestra to play and I said, 'List's *Préludes*'. The leader refused and I asked why. He said it was one of Hitler's favorites – I had no idea. Can you imagine?

T: Are there things that still bother you about the way your presidency ended?

RN: I can't lie to you – of course I wish it hadn't ended in resignation. That was a hell of an awful decision to make, but I did what I thought was best for the country at the time. That said, the lack of support from my colleagues . . . shook me. I'm the kind of guy who always wanted to know what people thought, but as things started going south – well, I guess they felt they had to cover their own behinds and I stopped hearing from them. I have no shame in admitting – I felt quite alone. Can you imagine that: the president of the United States feeling alone?

David Mitchell

interviews

SAMUEL JOHNSON
&
JAMES BOSWELL

DAVID MITCHELL, *an English author, was born in 1969.*

SAMUEL JOHNSON, *an English writer, poet, editor and lexicographer, died in 1784.*

JAMES BOSWELL, *the biographer of Samuel Johnson, died in 1795.*

SAMUEL JOHNSON: Reveal, Sir, your *why* and *wherefore*! Francis tells me you refuse to leave without speaking with Mr Boswell and myself?

DAVID MITCHELL: Dr Johnson! Granta sent me to do a dead interview and—

SJ: Who, pray, is Granta?

DM: It's a literary publisher from the twenty-first century. The editor won't let me go back to 2013 until I've got enough decent copy. I can't make it up either – he can hear every word we're saying, right now, through this little gizmo ...

SJ: Crazies, crazies. Why do *I* get all the crazies?

SERVANT: Doctor, perhaps I should carry this madman to the Thames that he may continue his ravings with the fishes?

DM: Ten questions, Doctor. Plus, the editor's authorized me to compensate you for your time. Up front, too. Quite a thing for Granta. They pay—

SJ: Sir, you are quite the Scaramouche! Do you presume that

Samuel Johnson, can be *bought and sold* like so many turnips?

DM: —one guinea per question.

SJ: Frank, what are you thinking? Our guest must be cold! Come in, my good – er . . . what did you say your name was?

Footsteps down a corridor. Creaky door. Crackling log fire.

SJ: *This* is James Boswell. A Scotchman, but, he admits, he can hardly be blamed for that. Mitchell's visiting us from the twenty-first century, Boswell, and his cruel master won't let him go home until he has spoken with us.

JAMES BOSWELL: Oh aye?

DM: An enormous pleasure, Mr Boswell. I read your *London Journal*. The bit where you catch VD from that actress. 'Too, too plain was Signor Gonorrhoea.' Laughed out loud!

JB: Delighted ye found it so funny.

Background snoring and groaning.

SJ: That insensible pile of youthful limbs on the settle, that's an engraver *manqué* called William Blake. I met him at the Turk's Head last winter. He visits me from time to time to borrow a shilling and to lick his wounds. *His* master abuses him for doing archangels instead of aristocrats. Poor William has imbibed of Swedenborg too freely.

DM: You, Boswell and William Blake! What a 'Buy Two Get One Free' offer! The face of eighteenth-century studies has changed!

SJ: Has it, Sir? Then let us sit down.

Sound of chair collapsing, cursing and a cackling Scot.

DM: Your famous three-legged chair. Funny. So, Dr Johnson, you are often lauded as one of the first professional writers, as opposed to playwright, or a rich man who wrote for pleasure. Your father was a bookseller in Lichfield—

SJ: Alas, not a successful one. His impecunity obliged me to abandon my studies at Oxford after only one year. One fellow student left me a pair of shoes outside my door, so worn were my own. The mortification, Sir, was more than I could bear.

DM: But since you arrived in London in 1737 you've written your way into a rather cosy corner. Your ex-pupil David Garrick staged your play *Irene*.

SJ: My play failed to please the town.

DM: *Irene* ran for nine nights. Not a flop. But then you produced hundreds of essays during the 1750s for *The Rambler*, *The Adventurer* and *The Idler*—

SJ: A man may write at any time, Sir, if he will set himself doggedly to it.

DM: I'll try to remember that. Your glorious makeovers of Juvenal's *Satires*, 'London' and 'The Vanity of Human Wishes', went down very well. Nine years were spent on the first English dictionary—

SJ: Not the first, Sir, merely the best.

DM: I could kick myself for not bringing you the OED on my

iPad. You'd *weep*. In 1759 came *Rasselas: Prince of Abyssinia*, a philosophical novel; and your editions of Shakespeare examined both the national bard's weaknesses *and* his strengths, arguably laying the foundations of modern literary criticism. Then in *Taxation No Tyranny* and *Thoughts on the Late Transactions Respecting Falkland's Islands* you venture into the political polemic. In 1775 you developed the genre of travel writing with your *Journey to the Western Islands of Scotland*, whose admirers included the King. In 1781 you laid one of the foundation stones of modern literary biography in *Lives of the Poets*. Samuel Johnson, this is your life!

JB: Was there a question lurking in that thicket?

DM: Got a bit carried away. My question is, Doctor, what do you consider to be your greatest achievement?

SJ: I dreamed, Sir, of being a poet and woke to find myself a lexicographer. That'll be one guinea, thank you. Do you know, the French Academy still will not own that my dictionary was the handiwork of but one man?

JB: Aye, and their Frenchie version required the exertions of *forty* members for *forty* years.

SJ: Sixteen hundred man-years! Mine took nine man-years! *That*, Sir, is the worth of an Englishman to a Frenchman! Nine of us to sixteen hundred of them!

DM: Sort of 'Up Yours, Delors!' then, eh?

Long awkward pause.

DM: Moving swiftly on. Women.

JB: Oho.

DM: You're a dark horse in this area. Not you, Mr Boswell, I've read your diaries. Doctor, you once said that women only have themselves to blame if their husbands have affairs.

SJ: Sir, a man will not, once in a hundred instances, leave his wife and go to a harlot, if his wife has not been negligent of pleasing him.

DM: But when Mr Boswell dared suggest that Lady Beauclerk should enjoy similar rights to her philandering Lord—

SJ: The lady to whom you refer, Sir, is, I think, very fit for a brothel.

DM: Quite. Then we have your opinion on women preachers. 'A woman's preaching is like a dog's walking on his hinder legs. It is not done well; but you are surprized to find it done at all.'

SJ: People have no sense of humour in your kingdom, Sir?

DM: Ah, but we have political correctness too. In your defence, critics point out how Prince Rasselas's sister, Princess Nekayeh, argues her corners as robustly as her brother. And since you arrived in London forty years ago as an 'adventurer of literature', you've given a leg-up to many proto-feminist—

JB: What's this? *Whose* legs?

DM: Oh, sorry. Blue Stockings. Female thinkers and writers. The doctor helped the careers of a number of them by raising subscriptions, writing prefaces and so on.

JB: Has he? Name me but one.

DM: Mrs Lennox, author of *The Female Quixote*; Fanny Burney, whose novels are still in print, by the way. And of course, the Doctor actually *lives* with Hester Thrale and her husband, even visiting France with them – until he dies and she marries that Italian, Piozzi, which hasn't happened yet. Sorry. Must stop doing that.

JB: I detest how that Thrale woman scribbles down every last *bon mot* ye drop, Doctor. The vulture's planning a *Life* if you ask me . . .

DM: So, Dr Johnson. What *is* your position on women intellectuals?

SJ: It is a paltry trick indeed, Sir, to deny women of the cultivation of their mental powers, and I think it is partly proof we are afraid of them, if we endeavour to keep them unarmed. One guinea, thank you.

DM: Are you afraid of women?

SJ: Nature has given women so much power that the law has wisely given them very little. A woman has such power between the ages of twenty-five and forty-five that she may tie a man to a post and whip him if she will. Another guinea.

DM: Only in very dodgy clubs.

SJ: I declare, Sir, your sentiments are as confounding as your lexicon! Are you by chance a Dutchman? Or, worse, late arrived from those Rascally Colonies? I make no secret of my disdain for that parcel of convicts. If they get anything more lenient than a collective hanging they ought to be content!

DM: The States, you mean? No, though I was in Australia in February. One hell of a flight. But perhaps we can bring in Mr Boswell now, to discuss your celebrated friendship. Mr Boswell's *Life of Johnson* is, by the 1820s, regarded as a peak of eighteenth-century letters. It earns him a first-class berth aboard the HMS *Immortality* and—

SJ: *What* are you saying? What is this? Boswell!

JB: I deny vehemently this saucy charge of literary parasitism, Sir!

DM: He won't write it till you're dead, Doctor. And it *is* a brilliant read. He gives away so much. That old Johnson–Boswell dynamic seems to be a real father–son thing.

SJ: Boswell *had* a father, Sir, when we met. Lord Auchinleck.

DM: But in 1761, the year you met, you told Boswell this: 'I am a man of the world. I live in the world, and I take, in some degree, the colour of the world as it moves along. Your father is a Judge in a remote part of the island, and all his notions are taken from the old world. Besides, Sir, there must also be a struggle between a father and son, while one aims at power and the other at independence.' Your wife, Elizabeth Porter, was twenty years your senior, so a son of your own was never really on the cards . . .

SJ: Dear Tetty. I still pray for her. I still observe her birthday, you know.

DM: . . . and when you *met* Mr Boswell's dad, jealousy – over James here – leaps off the page. You don't have to be Sigmund Freud to see some major displacements going on . . .

JB: I know not your Mr Freud, nor his Major Displacements, nor do I wish to. My veneration for Dr Johnson is no secret. Yes, as a son may venerate a beloved father. What of it? Do the young have no respect for their elders where ye hail from?

DM (*hesitates*): Not a lot, now you mention it. But your 'veneration' rather colours your account, don't you think? For example, what the Doctor told David Hume was that he didn't go to Garrick's green room because 'the white bubbies and the silk stockings of the actresses excite my genitals!' You *rewrote* this as, 'the silk stockings and the white bosoms of your actresses excite my amorous propensities'. If that's not whitewashing, give me another word for it. What do you think, Doctor?

SJ: Shush, shush, William's waking up . . .

DM: Do his eyes always rotate in opposite directions like that?

JB: Please no, not another 'vision' . . .

WILLIAM BLAKE: The burning logs in your fire, Doctor, chronicle all my wicked deeds.

SJ: Then ask them, Bill, why they do not chronicle your kind deeds.

WB: Urizen tells me I must leave now and eat eels. Good morning.

Footsteps leave the room. Awkward pause.

JB: I fear the boy is bound for the madhouse, Doctor.

SJ: The madhouse if fortune smiles, Sir, or publishing his own poetry if not.

DM: I hate to hurry, but the Granta Device is a pay-by-the-minute deal. I attended a symposium about you a few years back, Doctor. One lecture was called 'The Soul of Samuel Johnson – Right or Left?' Academics in my time would like to know where *you* position your soul?

SJ: To the right and left, Sir, of what?

DM: The political spectrum. Conservatives and Liberals.

SJ: If, by 'Liberals', you refer to Whigs, this matter may be settled in a trice. Whiggism is a negation of all principle! In matters of religion, in matters of politics, I am an unswerving friend of the established order and a humble servant of His Majesty George the Third.

DM: Ah yes, your pension. The crown pays you £300 per annum, yet in your dictionary we read: 'Pension: An allowance made to any one without an equivalent. In England it is generally understood to mean pay given to a state hireling for treason to his country.'

SJ: I accepted the pension on an assurance that my award was not for what was expected of me *in the future*, but rather, for what I had achieved *in the past*.

JB: And ye can deposit *that* where the sun shines not.

DM: O-kay, I guess we'd file you under 'Unapologetic Conservative' in my own century, then.

SJ: I am glad on't! I am a friend to subordination, as most conducive to the happiness of society. There is a reciprocal pleasure in governing and being governed.

DM: Would you say that if you were a peasant eking out a short, illiterate, shivering, miserable life in a turf hut, like the ones you saw in the Hebrides?

SJ: I trust, Sir, I am not to be blamed for each instance of misgovernance in this broad kingdom?

DM: But you don't agree, the poor might need to persuade their governors to govern them a little better?

SJ: Oh? You advocate a Universal Suffrage, perhaps, for the unlettered to pick their masters on a whim?

DM: It'll take over a hundred years, but yes, it happens. On the other hand, you sometimes come over as pretty Lib-Dem, if not downright Labour. 'A decent provision of the poor is the true test of civilization.' Your anti-slavery stand is way ahead of your time. At dinner once in Oxford you proposed a toast, 'Here's to the next insurrection of the negroes in the West Indies!'

SJ: Plum-duff plantation – fat faces make me puke, that's the truth on't! No powers can be the conscience of Europe. But should one therefore embrace sedition? Revolution? The Chinaman says, 'Better a hundred years of tyranny than a single afternoon of anarchy.'

DM: See? You're impossible to pin down.

SJ: The truth is not a butterfly, Sir. Truth is evasive of pins. Now, I shall leave you to Boswell's tender mercies. I am one who with tea amuses the evening, with tea solaces the midnight and with tea welcomes the morning. But I declare, Sir, it goes straight through me.

Clunky footsteps. Door closing.

JB (*hisses*): Right, ye scoundrel, alone at last! I know not by what devilry ye gain access to my innermost meditations, but no lunatic licks *me* with impunity!

DM: Oi! Get off my guineas!

Clatters. Grunts. Cries of pain.

JB: Oho! What is this? Your Granta guineas, Sir, are minted in
     1788!
DM *(speaking through crushed windpipe)*: So what?
JB: Sir, the year is 1782! Why, this should earn ye twenty years in
     the forger's jail! But I'll do my best to push for thirty!
DM: Oh, *bugger.* Granta! Beam me up!
JB: Nor will ye be needing *this* box of devilry where ye be bound!
DM: No, Boswell, not my Granta Device!

Mocking Boswellian laughter.

DM: No! NOT THE FIRE! I CAN'T GET BACK WITHOUT—

Transmission ends.

Granta would be grateful to hear from any person or persons who
can help us contact David Mitchell. His publishers are getting
edgy about the deadline for his next book and we would like to
send him his cheque.

John Burnside

interviews

RACHEL CARSON

JOHN BURNSIDE, *a Scottish author and poet, was born in 1955.*

RACHEL CARSON, *an American marine biologist and conservationist whose book* Silent Spring *(1962) was fundamental to the global environmental movement, died in 1964.*

On a clear, crisp Sunday afternoon in February 2013, I invited Rachel Carson over from the afterlife (which is just a mile or so into the next parish), adding that, if she was willing, I would very much like to ask her a few questions about the relevance of her work to the environmental problems we face today over a pot of Orange Pekoe and a plate of my home-made scones. She kindly agreed. What follows is not so much an interview as an account of a wide-ranging conversation that, for reasons of economy, has been slightly edited.

JOHN BURNSIDE: I suppose the obvious question to begin with is, how much do you think has changed since *Silent Spring*?

RACHEL CARSON: Ah. The obvious question. Which is usually not very interesting. Though, in this case, we could note how very successful big business has been in its manipulation of the 'green agenda'. Of course, the dice were loaded from the start (government's main purpose is to support corporate and land-management interests, after all), but they really

have been as clever as they are ruthless and they have made
devious use of climate-change science in particular.

JB: Really? I thought most businesses denied climate change—

RC: Oh, no. That phase is almost over. Now, too many people
understand that things have been going very wrong for a very
long time, so the powers that be have been compelled to erect
a complex edifice of misinformation, misdirection, public
relations, dubious consultations and supposed 'community'
schemes, supplemented, when necessary, by outright lies, to
sell their agenda. Your current shorthand for this, I believe, is
greenwashing. As it happens, I had some interest in the climate
question back in the 1950s, but I had to put that aside for
Silent Spring. Today, you have a plethora of 'silent spring'-type
issues, old and new, from the misrepresentation of science
by business interests in order to sell unrealistic and environmentally destructive 'green' energy solutions (massive wind
turbines, biomass, etc.), through deflection of attention from
species loss and ocean acidification (fortunes aren't made in
those fields, I'm afraid), to the same old story with pesticides,
most recently neonicotinoids, which do seem to pose a grave
threat to bees.

JB: I'm not sure I understand – are you saying things are just as
bad as they were in 1962?

RC: Not at all. Things are much worse now. Especially in the
oceans, which were, after all, my special area of interest.

JB: But more people think of themselves as being 'green' today
than ever before—

RC: That's all well and good. And many of them will be decent, honest citizens, concerned for the future of their children, but they are being systematically misinformed. I was compelled to write *Silent Spring* by 'ordinary' citizens who felt that a great wrong was being committed by the agrichemical business and they needed someone to speak out on their behalf. What is important here is that they were just concerned citizens, with no particular ideology or commercial interests. They just loved the natural world and wanted to protect it. Now, however, there is an orthodoxy about being green and climate change and an ill-informed self-righteousness about 'saving the planet' – and orthodoxy is easily manipulated by the corrupt and the self-interested, who will embrace any rhetoric whatsoever to get what they want. It reminds me of those flim-flam men who turned up at revival meetings in the old days, preying on the faithful. The faithful are not stupid; it's just that they *want* so much to believe. They want to think they are doing their bit to save the earth. But you can't save anything under the present system – and every lite-green compromise and gesture, from wind turbines to municipal recycling, helps perpetuate that system.

JB: So why do you think we are we settling for what you call 'lite-green'?

RC: Obviously, real change is difficult; it requires rigour and imagination. But it's also the case that the business people are even more devious now. This was one of the unwanted consequences of *Silent Spring*: they learned from that small victory and vowed never to let it happen again. Think how much money agribusiness and pharmaceutical and energy companies spend on advertising and PR. Not to mention the money and assets that change hands behind the scenes, via party donations and research foundations and the like. Or the propaganda disseminated in schools by, say, energy or food companies, who provide information packs and site visits to make their argument to the unprepared. The backroom pressures and persuasions exerted upon broadcasters and the media. This was wholly reprehensible when big oil and coal were the guilty parties; it's just as reprehensible when 'renewable' energy companies and *soi-disant* green manufacturers do it.

JB: Well, at least they don't resort to the methods they used to discredit your work—

RC: Oh, I'm not sure that's true. Not at all. I would like to think that those tactics were a thing of the past, but I'm afraid they aren't. If anything, those commercial interests whose profits depend on having a free hand to denature the environment have become more insidious than ever. The methods may have changed, but the message is the same. After *Silent Spring*, it wasn't just the men from big business who attacked me. William Darby, chief biochemist at Vanderbilt School of Medicine, dismissed me as a spokesperson for 'organic gardeners, the anti-fluoride leaguers, the worshippers of natural foods, those who cling to the philosophy of a vital principle and other pseudo-science faddists' (I would love to say he's a little embarrassed about that now, but for some reason he's never turned up in my section of the afterlife). Well, that was bad enough, but at least I was in good company. Ezra Taft Benson, Secretary of Agriculture, got a touch more personal, saying I was probably a communist, and wondering why a 'spinster was so worried about genetics'. Come to think of it, I haven't seen Mr Benson in this part of the afterlife either . . .

This is ancient history, in some respects, but it's also relevant now. Words can be used to talk about the richness and beauty of the natural world and the importance of the balance of nature; however, those powerful gentlemen gave me a two-year education in the various nefarious uses of language: as bludgeon, as insinuation, as misinformation and, when necessary, as out-and-out lies. What upset me most wasn't the personal attacks, it was the suggestion that, because I was a woman, I had no claim to scientific understanding and, because I was not affiliated to some institution at the time of publication, I was a dilettante. As if any embedded institution would have allowed me to say what I said . . . But then, that was the point. If you're not a member of their club, you're supposed to remain silent. That's why we need other, independent groups to question every commercial act and government decree, to question *everything*, in fact, carefully, consistently and with the determination that comes of refusing to compromise the interests of nature, which is to say *all* our interests.

JB: But surely there are organizations that do that now, in no small measure thanks to your example.

RC: There may well be. But even here, as with everything else, there are those you can trust and those you can't.

JB: For example?

RC: Well, how about something that is happening in your own backyard?

JB: Perfect.

RC: This item, from the *Sunday Herald* of Glasgow, 10 January 2010, tells how a plan to 'string giant pylons 137 miles down Scotland's spine ... ended with a split in the environmental movement like no other'. I'll read on, because the crux of the piece is in the next paragraph or so: 'On one side are those who care passionately about wild land and protecting the country's stunningly beautiful landscapes. They include Ramblers Scotland, The John Muir Trust and The Association for the Protection of Rural Scotland. On the other are those who strongly believe the sacrifice is essential to give the nation a clean, safe and climate-friendly energy future. They include Friends of the Earth Scotland, WWF Scotland and The Green Party.'

Now, it is hard not to notice the manner in which this story is being reported. The first group 'care passionately', while the second 'strongly believe'; the first group are only concerned with pretty scenery, the second are ready to make a sacrifice to fight climate change and give the nation a clean, safe future (though how 137 miles of high-voltage power lines cutting through a national park makes anyone any safer is beyond me). The article goes on to mention, then dismiss, public concern over the 'inconclusive but worrying risks from electromagnetic radiation' from these pylons. ('Inconclusive' is a favoured term with the business green lobby; there is never conclusive evidence for anything until it is too late, because nobody funds that kind of *independent* research.) I could go on; the article is riddled with slanted arguments, but I'll stick to this: according to our correspondent, the main cause of the split is 'the increasingly urgent need to cut the pollution that scientists claim is disrupting the climate', a statement that, while he puts us in no doubt as to which side he is on, overlooks the glaringly obvious fact that installing 137 miles of power lines will do *nothing at all* to cut pollution.

Yet, in spite of the slanted reporting, in spite of the reporter's clear disapproval of the 'emotive and headline-grabbing' language used by 'the landscape groups' (ah, now we know how trivial their concerns are; they're probably a bunch of Sunday painters in floppy hats and sentimental tree-huggers), what I see here is that there are some so-called environmentalist groups who are willing to compromise with an environmentally damaging commercial–political axis and others who are not. This may be for a variety of reasons, but 'by their fruits ye shall know them', so I am more inclined to trust the John Muir folks than the 'bulldogs for the energy lobby' (as one journalist called them) at Friends of the Earth. Why? Because, while no mention is made of it here, we know there are clear concerns regarding bird mortality and overhead power lines and, while *independent* studies are uncommon, both sides must be aware of the work of such observers as Kjetil Bevanger, of the Norwegian Institute for Nature Research, whose work in this field suggests that 'an alarmingly large number of species with endangered and vulnerable status are identified among the victims [of mortality due to collisions with power lines]'. But, once again, the birds are forgotten, even by *The Herald*'s environment correspondent – and with the bulldogs' help, this 'needless and myopic act of vandalism' is going ahead.

JB: Same journalist?

RC: Yes.

JB: I think I read the piece. Didn't he also say 'by allowing this kind of project to go ahead through the heart of a national park, the Scottish executive has shown that everything is up for grabs'?

RC: They had already shown their true colours during the Menie affair. Where is the independent public inquiry into that particular scandal? I have to say, you really don't do local democracy very well in Scotland. Perhaps it's your feudal heritage...

JB: So how do we counter this alliance of greed and bulldog ideology?

RC: What we need is a mass coalition of politically sceptical, not-for-sale people who refuse to tolerate a diet of weak poisons, a home in insipid surroundings, a circle of acquaintances who are not quite their enemies, the noise of motors – I am repeating myself here, but in all honesty, who wants to live in a world that is just not quite fatal? Such a movement would not form a business or a party, they wouldn't want to own or control anything, they would simply oppose any measure or product that was not demonstrably in the interests of life itself, wherever it occurs . . .

JB: A party of permanent opposition, perhaps?

RC: Perhaps.

JB: I like that idea. It reminds me of the old alchemist's adage: 'The adept owns nothing, but has the use of everything . . .'

RC: Well, the wording's rather odd, but that's part of it, certainly, because – well, we certainly do like to own things, don't we? Not just property, but ideas and the sense of righteousness. I can't help thinking we'd all be a good deal better off if ownership were either properly communal or non-existent. Though I suppose that amounts to the same thing. Yet in spite of, or is it because of, all this ownership, we make such tawdry uses of the natural world. What kind of a tawdry mind is it that makes mountains, rivers, shorelines, oceans, lakes, people into *resources*?

JB: I see we're back to language again. Don't you think a word like 'resources' could be used quite innocently, in certain circumstances?

RC: It depends on the context. But in most cases, probably not. It's like ownership. If we talk about ownership without understanding that to own is both a form of theft and a foolish illusion, then we have further to travel before we can do justice to life itself, human and non-human. Until you get the gist of the old Sufi saying that a person only owns what she cannot lose in a shipwreck, then you will never have the proper and full use of anything, right down to your own body.

JB: It sounds like the afterlife has made you more radical than you were in life. Or were you moving in that direction anyway? I've often wondered about what you might have done had you lived longer.

RC: Well, that was a long time ago. But I can say that I had a wonderful life and, as to death, well, many died a good deal younger than me. My sister Marian was just forty when she departed. Yet over the years I have come to see that, while the process of dying might be painful, death itself is a mercy, at least for the individual who dies. Or rather, it's a mercy compared to the alternative. Imagine how tedious individual immortality would be. But the drama of life on earth, a drama in which we are, not immortal, but eternal participants, goes on without the individual instances of the species to which we are so attached. That is the gift any life scientist receives, from the moment she first begins working in the field – to know that it is life itself that matters, the flow of it, the true natural history. Then, paradoxically, the perishable instances of life to which we are attached become ever more precious, ever more tender, and that realization might well be the most precious gift of all. Certainly, that should be the fundamental principle of all our politics: *If it harms life, don't do it.* What could more fundamental than that?

ZZ Packer

interviews

MONSIEUR DE SAINT-GEORGE

ZZ PACKER, *an American author, was born in 1973.*

MONSIEUR DE SAINT-GEORGE, *known as 'The Black Mozart', died in 1799.*

The famous son of Guillaume-Pierre Tavernier de Boullogne and his black slave and consort Nanon, the violin virtuoso and celebrated master composer, the director of the Olympic Society of Concerts, the finest fencer and swordsman in the kingdom, the Lieutenant of the Hunt to the duc d'Orléans (aka Philippe *Égalité*), black Jacobin, the first black Mason, the first black colonel in the French Army, the incomparable Monsieur de Saint-George, Joseph Boulogne, also known as the Chevalier de Saint-George.

ZZP: Alain Guédé has written a book about you, rehabilitating your name – and fame – but how strange that you should have been forgotten in the first place. You were, it seems, the inspiration for Alexandre Dumas' musketeers, that's how fine a swordsman you were. You regularly swam one-armed across the Seine – for show! You were the best violinist in all of Paris, then you composed music and were once even referred to as 'The Black Mozart'. I'm finding it hard to believe that such a man has been forgotten.

MDS-G: What good is fame when one is dead? For a time, right before the Revolution, I was indeed the greatest fencer and swordsman in all of France, and became first violinist in La Popelinière's orchestra under the direction of the great Gossec, before becoming a composer and an orchestra director in my own right. And also, you forget, the world's first black Mason and the first ever black colonel in the French Army. Should I say that I was the first 'black' friend of the Prince of Wales? The first black music tutor to Marie Antoinette? These seem diminishments, not accomplishments. Any time one is deemed 'the black' *anything*, they mean to place you – by displacing you. To live as another's footnote: *that* is death.

ZZP: Well, you didn't *have* to . . .

MDS-G: Actually, yes, I did. When one is born a slave, such as my mother, one must survive, and find the most ingenious ways of doing so. When one is born into a titled noble family, such as my father, one must find ways of maintaining one's nobility – which, like sterling, requires constant polishing.

ZZP: Your father had a noble title, yet you don't possess it.

MDS-G: No, I do not.

ZZP: Would you care to elaborate?

MDS-G: I do not care to, yet I will. Roman law dictates that the child shall inherit and follow the condition of the mother, and my mother was a black slave. It was thus illegal for my father to give me his name, or for me to take it. My father's property was next to that of his distant relative Georges Bologne de Saint-Georges, in the district of Saint-Georges. I am thus named from the district, not my father. My father, though a white Frenchman, went to great pains to recognize my mother as his wife.

ZZP: Did she ...

MDS-G: Of course she still bore witness to the cane mills, where slaves worked shifts to exhaustion and, inevitably, children fell between the crushers that extracted the juice ... There was a special hook that hung over the machines to slice off hands and arms that got caught in the works, lest the whole body get caught as well and the slave be pulped like paper through the rollers. That would have been a double loss.

ZZP: You say he went to great pains to recognize your mother as his wife, yet he sought his fortune as a slave owner.

MDS-G: A plantation owner.

ZZP: Still, he owned a plantation and a plantation's holdings are not merely the land or the buildings, but the human property – slaves.

MDS-G: The royals were, as you say, hemorrhaging money. And who better to give a transfusion of money than a successful businessman? And so a good healthy transfusion of money could be exchanged for a transfusion of 'good blood'.

ZZP: And he married another wife – a white Frenchwoman.

MDS-G: He could not re-establish himself in French society with my mother, Nanon, who'd once been a slave. When Guillaume-Pierre Tavernier de Boullogne – my father – returned to Paris with his fortune, he needed to establish his title once more. In order for me to have the best of everything – violin lessons, fencing at La Boëssière's school for young gentlemen, a chariot in the English style, riding lessons and proper society – he had to present well. So, yes, he married another.

Does that make him – or me – a Monarchist? Of course, when you've been the violin tutor of Marie Antoinette, you could be mistaken for a royalist. Let me say this: I did not die by guillotine, though many thousands did. In fact I was – and am, if I may say so – a Jacobin, in so far as an artist can 'be' anything . . .

The royals were wrong, the Jacobins were wrong. Can the *Palais* continue to exist by extorting the people, their so-called Third Estate inferiors? No. It is wrong. Can the Jacobins, fighting such injustice, kill injustice with a guillotine? No. The just *Révolution française* is followed by *la Terreur*.

ZZP: The French are always so philosophical.

MDS-G: Dear one, I am Francophone, not French. I was never allowed to forget that. But yes, philosophy, the Enlightenment taught us, creates as many shadowy umbras as it does radiant coronas. You are welcome to the metaphor.

ZZP: You not only tutored Marie Antoinette, you served as a model for a very famous writer, Alexandre Dumas, the son of Thomas-Alexandre 'Dumas' Davy de La Pailleterie, a mulatto from Saint-Domingue . . .

MDS-G: Alexandre was not a notable fencer, though he attended the same school, La Boëssière's, as I – and it was the absolute finest school of its day, and he the undisputed master, until, of course, I surpassed him. Alexandre was quite bitter that his father was never as handsome or as noted as I.

ZZP: Do you believe Dumas – the Younger – based *The Three Musketeers* on you?

MDS-G: I was indeed a musketeer, having mastered horsemanship at the riding school at the Tuileries. However, the musketeers were nobles, and though my father was considered a noble, I had no title. Remaining a musketeer depended upon the sons of the nobility allowing me to do so, and they did not allow it.

Years earlier, one of the musketeers – an idiot by the name of La Morlière – had complained *sotto voce* about competing against a 'half-caste'. I went at him with every fiber of my being, tossed him across the room and, before the night was over, whipped him soundly. So it was jealousy, pure and simple. I'd bedded those they'd wished to but could not, or those they'd bedded poorly. These 'sons of the nobility' could not bear for me to be a musketeer beside them, despite my being superior to them in every way. So I served in the lesser King's Guard, as a gendarme.

ZZP: Yet you must admit the similarities . . .

MDS-G: This d'Artagnan, as I understand him, duels with anyone who insults him. Soon adventures ensue with the queen and her cuckold husband and a landlord's wife trying to get the landlord to London because of Cardinal Richelieu . . . I did go off to London, as d'Artagnan did, and had many adventures, but that was with the duke's son, who chose the name Philippe *Égalité*. I was saved from squalor when one Madame de Montesson, wife of the duc d'Orléans, second in power only to the king, invited me to take up an apartment in the

Palais-Royal, and she did charm the once-cuckolded duke . . .

But there the similarity ends, as I eventually became a colonel in the French Army – I was *not* a royalist or a monarchist. I fought for the Revolution, and, as a man of color, believed in it. It was I who led the Society of the Friends of the Blacks, I who ended up in prison, for eighteen months, stripped of my rank, all because the Revolution became the Terror, with nearly 17,000 decapitated at the guillotine. Was this d'Artagnan capering along, until he was accused of being a *girondiste* and relieved of this life?

ZZP: I'm so sorry. Were you sent – did you succumb – to the guillotine?

MDS-G: Of course not. There were too many people who wanted a black man dead to give them my head so easily! During the Revolution I strove to keep the fortress of Lille from falling to the forces of Cobourg and Dumouriez. And for that I was imprisoned.

ZZP: So you died in prison?

MDS-G: The Committee of Public Safety – *the Terroristes* – finally decided that I was a revolutionary after all. But by the time they'd decided such a thing, a new law had been enacted – to flush out any possible royalists in the ranks. Anyone who had not been in active service on such and such a date was immediately suspended . . .

However, if I could not direct or play music or lead my *chausseurs*, I thought I'd work with my brethren in the Isles. I went to Saint-Domingue on behalf of the Republic to help abolish slavery. Napoleon, the savage, reinstated it. I was 'a Frenchman' to the mulattos – the irony! My sentence: to be hanged.

ZZP: So you died by hang—

MdS-G: I escaped, of course.

ZZP: What of your music? Your compositions?

MdS-G: What of them? Once I was finally 'redeemed' and considered to be on the side of the Revolution, none of the *émigré* patrons of the arts – monarchists all – would dare to support me upon their return to Paris. So those much lesser lights went on to glory while I did not.

But it could have been worse, *ma chérie*. Had I received the Palais-Royal position, serving as director of music for Marie-Antoinette, I'd be dead.

ZZP: But, you *are* dead.

MdS-G: I'd be dead at the blade of the guillotine, cut down long before '99. Philippe *Égalité*, who named me Lieutenant of the Hunt and who bankrolled the Revolution as well – guillotined . . .

Yet I live. Gustave Dugazon – son of the *incroyable* diva Louise-Rosalie Dugazon . . . my music lived on through him. But of course she could never tell the world he was mine.

That, *ma chérie*, is the way things are, and have always been. You must live in one world and love in another. One is black and white – the other color and music. To confuse the two – as I once did – is nothing but folly.

Michel Faber

interviews

MARCEL DUCHAMP

MICHEL FABER, *author of* The Crimson Petal and the White, *was born in 1960.*

MARCEL DUCHAMP, *a French-American artist, died peacefully in 1968.*

MICHEL FABER: You've been called the Daddy of Dada, the Grandpa of Pop, the Conceiver of Conceptual Art . . .

MARCEL DUCHAMP: These epithets make me sound like Methuselah. I never wanted to father anything. Art is not about legacies.

MF: What *is* it about?

MD: Sudden realizations.

MF: Yet you are now widely regarded as the most influential artist of the twentieth century.

MD: Influential? I'm not so sure. There is a character called Marcel Duchamp described in history books, whom poseurs dutifully add to a list of significant personages in their discourse. This is not the same thing as being confronted by a work of art that makes you dizzy with confusion, that makes you quarrel with your companions and run into the street blushing.

MF: Wouldn't you accept credit, though, for empowering modern artists? You argued that art is whatever the artist says it is, not what critics say it is.

MD: Once upon a time, all artists were secure in that conviction. Do you think Caravaggio or Bosch, or for that matter the primitive who carved the Willendorf Venus, was in the least worried what critics thought? I would have liked to steer modern artists back towards that sort of courage, but I failed miserably. The artists of today are addicted to criticism. They have ceased to care what happens or doesn't happen when an anonymous person stands before their work. They hanker only for the reviews.

MF: Aren't you being a bit harsh? Many modern artists seem to be living out your principle that the viewer is the co-creator of a work of art, that the viewer completes the process.

MD (*after a moment's reflection*): True. You must forgive my jadedness. It's a deplorable trait, which I was never guilty of until 1969. The trouble is, I really have seen it all before. Indeed, I invented most of it.

MF: Yet people can still be shocked by art.

MD: Give me an example.

MF: David Sherry sewing planks of balsa wood to his feet.

MD: What this provokes in the public is not shock. It is queasiness. The sight of an Englishman eating baked beans can produce the same effect. Especially if he has a moustache.

MF: Speaking of moustaches ... let's talk about your famous work of 1919, *L.H.O.O.Q.*, in which you added a moustache and beard to Leonardo's *Mona Lisa*. Are you aware that Jake and Dinos Chapman have recently modified the engravings of Goya in the same way?

MD: I wouldn't say 'the same way'. My defacing of the *Mona Lisa* was deliberately amateurish, as if a schoolboy had done it as a prank while the gallery attendant's back was turned. It was intended to challenge people's notions of the sanctity of artworks, the value that they unquestioningly put on them.

MF: It wasn't intended as a ready-made? Or as an androgyne symbol?

MD: Certainly. These were additional amusements for me. But the main purpose was to shock. And for people to ask themselves why they were shocked.

MF: The Chapmans' defacing of Goya shocked people too.

MD: I doubt it, and I would also challenge the word 'defacing'. To add carefully executed clown faces to prints of Goya's drawings is a diverting game, but no one imagines, even for an instant, that someone has interfered with the originals. The whole exercise is like those magazine advertisements where Michelangelo's Adam holds a telephone or whatever. It is a cheeky *homage*, which does not challenge the superior merit of the original, and indeed invites the viewer to be reminded of the exalted heritage. This is not what I was saying with *L.H.O.O.Q.* I was saying, 'What is this icon to us? Why do we continue to genuflect before it?'

MF: Such pieces as Tracey Emin's bed and Martin Creed's light turning on and off genuinely caused outrage. Wasn't that a modern manifestation of the same controversy you provoked when you exhibited the urinal in 1917?

MD: What shocked people about *Fountain* was the mere fact that

I exhibited it and called it art. What shocked people about Tracey Emin's bed and Martin Creed's light was the financial value assigned to them. Creed made the public furious, yes, but not because he dared call his installation art; people are indifferent to such statements now. They resented him being paid a great deal of money, and grinning all over his face.

MF: Can you understand such a reaction?

MD: Well, the boy must get money from somewhere, who cares how and where from? Would people rather he was stacking tins of food in a supermarket?

MF: Perhaps they would. Especially if they worked in a supermarket themselves, earning less in a year than Martin Creed earned at a stroke.

MD: Oh, this idea of fair wages for a quantifiable amount of work: it's so depressingly bourgeois. It presupposes that you are accountable to God, that He will pat you on the head for the hours you put in and the suffering you endured. Think of a painting like *Le Sacre* by Jacques-Louis David, depicting the coronation of Napoleon. Dozens of officiaries, all rendered in photographic detail. It must have taken David months to complete, each painstaking brushstroke bringing the picture closer to utter ghastliness. To this sort of dismal labour, the average bourgeois would gladly award prizes.

MF: You said in 1913 that painting was all washed up. In recent years, we've seen a revival of interest in works on canvas. Jenny Saville, Chris Ofili . . .

MD: Let me tell you a story! When my urinal was exhibited at the

Society of Independent Artists in New York City, one of the board members became very angry. He wanted to know if the Society would next accept a canvas with horse manure on it. I don't think his imagination quite stretched to elephants.

MF: I'm surprised you're familiar with . . .

MD: I keep up with everything, dear boy. I would have liked to get an Ofili imported up here, but animal-waste products are prohibited. You wouldn't *believe* what is prohibited here. If Jackson Pollock wants to go on a bender, he has to nip down to Limbo.

MF: So is there art in Heaven?

MD: Certainly there is art. The whole damn place is decorated with Rothkos. All very lovely, I'm sure, but it's enough to make you want to kill yourself.

MF: You wouldn't like some of your own work exhibited there? *The Bride Stripped Bare*, for example?

MD: Broken glass is not allowed in Heaven. Nothing imperfect is allowed, it's built along Platonic lines. Hopelessly fascist, in other words.

MF: You've been quite dismissive of several artists during our conversation so far, which has surprised me. In your earlier career, you were known for your generosity. For example, you defended Dalí and De Chirico when Breton expelled them from the Surrealist movement.

MD (*sighs*): Art is always in trouble when it regards itself as a club from which members can be expelled. I was defending art as much as I was defending Dalí and De Chirico, who were good friends of mine. I don't get along so well with Dalí nowadays. He came up to join us in 1989 and still hasn't washed or changed his clothing. You can imagine. And De Chirico is still painting the same piazza with the reclining statue and the little girl with the hoop. There are now several thousand of the wretched things piled up. If they hit the marketplace, they would be worth about twenty euros apiece.

MF: And in Heaven, they keep their value?

MD: In Heaven, nothing has value. It is the ultimate triumph for a man of my philosophies, and the ultimate humiliation, too.

MF: Can you tell me, apart from Rothko, what is God's taste in art?

MD: He and Monet are very chummy. They spend all day discussing water lilies, sunsets, flowers, the infinite gradations of light. They are like a couple newly in love. They chortle and tickle each other under the chin. I would like to slap them both with a dead fish. This, too, is not permitted.

MF: Let's talk about sex. In 1920 you created a female alter ego, Rrose Sélavy. You signed a number of your art objects in her name and most of your literary works. You even dressed in drag. I'm sure you're aware that gender and sexuality issues have become central to art in recent decades. How would you say your Rrose Sélavy persona reflected your own sexuality?

MD: Are you asking me if I was a transvestite or a homosexual?

MF: Yes, I suppose so.

MD: I think you should ask Rrose Sélavy that question. Only she knows the answer.

MF: Much was made of the fact that your most famous painting, *Nude Descending a Staircase*, was not identifiably male or female.

MD (*snorts impatiently*): This gadget you have placed on the table between us – this tape recorder. Is it male or female?

MF: Neither. It's a machine.

MD: We are all machines, my boy. If I exhibit this tape recorder of yours and call it *The Virgin Mary*, it becomes female. These three buttons can be nipples and a clitoris. This interior becomes the womb, housing the cassette which is Jesus, otherwise known as Logos, the incarnation of the Word. I'm sure we can extemporize more in this vein, given time and a few drinks. But what I've come up with in twenty seconds, cold sober, is enough to keep us occupied.

MF: People who knew you when you were … uh … before you moved to Heaven, described you as a man who was philosophical in the deepest sense of that word, rather like John Cage. You and he seemed to share not just an artistic agenda, but a serenity, an open-mindedness, a sense of fun. You seem more irritable now.

MD: Well, it's forty-five years since I had a smoke. Would you mind if I … ?

MF: It's not actually allowed in this building.

MD (*sighs deeply*): As above, so below.

MF: One final question. If you were in a position to collect the work of one modern artist, whose would you choose?

MD: Jack Vettriano.

MF: Jack Vettriano?

MD: Jack Vettriano.

MF: You are joking, surely?

MD (*smiling*): I've never been more serious.

MF: But he is loathed by every credible art critic in the world. What ... uh ... attracts ... ?

MD: I have no interest in his technique. Who cares about brush-strokes? Art critics should know that this discussion was rendered defunct a hundred years ago. The thing about Vettriano is, the characters in his paintings know how to dress. The women wear proper silk stockings, such as I myself would wear if I were in a Rrose Sélavy mood. The men wear smart trousers, crisp shirts, decent suits. Hats, even.

MF: I ... I must confess I'm shocked.

MD: There you are, my boy. I haven't lost my touch.

Rebecca Miller

interviews

THE MARQUIS DE SADE

REBECCA MILLER, *an American film director,*
screenwriter and novelist, was born in 1962.

THE MARQUIS DE SADE, *a French aristocrat,*
revolutionary politician and libertine, died peacefully
in his sleep in 1814.

Using an exciting new app, 'Time Warp', I reached the Marquis
in the Bastille on 2 July, in the year 1789, by which time he had
been imprisoned for twelve years by special order of the king,
under charges of debauchery and excessive libertinage. He was
forty-nine years old.

REBECCA MILLER: Dear Marquis de Sade, I am a writer, assigned
    to interview you. Would you be so kind as to give me a bit of
    your time? Best regards, R. Miller.
MARQUIS DE SADE: Who gave you my address?
RM: Inspector Buhot.
MDS: Fuck off. How would that philistine Buhot know a writer?
RM: It's to do with your release.
MDS: The true libertine loves even the punishment he receives.
    The gallows itself would be for me a voluptuous throne, and
    there would I face death by relishing the pleasure of expiring
    a victim of my crimes.
RM: You really relish being a prisoner?

MDS: What do *you* think? It's hell. I'm talking about an ideal. You are an informer, I assume.

RM: No. I am here to interview you about your life, your character, your writing. Buhot will see none of it.

MDS: What do you know about my writing?

RM: You are famous.

MDS: I am *in*famous, my man. Why should I have a correspondence with you? Can you help my release?

RM: Your release will be imminent.

MDS: Tell me any date for an end to this, for to set no limit is deliberately to reduce me to the depths of despair. Tell me, tell me, or I will smash my head against the walls that contain me!

RM: I promise you will be out of prison within the month.

MDS: I can't take it anymore. I will agree to the interview. I hope you are not an idiot.

RM: I am curious about your mother, among other things.

MDS: That bitch? Who cares about her?

RM: The people who sent me.

MDS: I have gone beyond believing a word anyone says. My own mother-in-law has laid the traps that destroyed my life. Mme de Montreuil.

RM: Tell me about her.

MDS: Mme de Montreuil is an infernal monster, a venomous beast, a trollop of a mother. I write my letters to her in blood.

RM: Your imprisonment is not punishment for your own crimes?

MDS: What crimes? I've been in prison for twelve years. I never killed anyone. Paris is filled with libertines worse than me.

This exchange is a waste of time. I must do something about my hemorrhoids.

RM: My deadline is tomorrow. If we could just go through a few more questions?

MDS: Fire away, then.

RM: You have a fascinating psychological profile. We would call it an inverse Oedipus Complex. Where you hate your mother and want to be close to your father. You went on to hate all mother figures, and motherhood itself.

MDS: What is this twaddle?

RM: What is your first memory?

MDS: Getting furious at another boy, in the courtyard of our home.

RM: Why?

MDS: No idea. Who are these people who say they can help get me out?

RM: Important people.

MDS: My hemorrhoids are killing me.

RM: Have you tried sitz baths?

MDS: If you could procure for me a certain little tube perforated with holes. One pumps water through it. Very soothing. I have asked my wife for one in my letters but she is refusing to contact me now. She has abandoned me.

RM: I will do my best to find one. Your wife, Renée-Pélagie. She stood by you for years, through your first arrests, scandals, flights from the law, show trials, the seduction of her own sister. Was she shocked by your proclivities when you were first married?

MDS: She was a blank slate, so she didn't know what to expect.

RM: You mean to say she shares your tastes?

MDS: She has shared my life.

RM: I know about your castle, the Château de Lacoste. I know you two holed up there for a winter after you escaped from prison. You and your wife hired some very young servants – teenagers, some of them – and then imprisoned them in the castle. You beat them, engaged in sexual acts. I know you were up to all sorts of stuff there, but no one knows how much Renée-Pélagie was involved. No one knows if she participated. I personally would be very interested to know.

MDS: Your information is foul. I refuse to go on.

RM: Do you want to get out of prison or not?

Five hours pass with no word from the Marquis. I worry I have lost him.

MDS: That winter at La Coste, my wife and I lived a simple, almost monastic life. We ate dinner at three o'clock. I spent the afternoon in my study, working.

RM: Working on what?

MDS: Theater.

RM: Theater to be played out in the castle?

MDS: I had it all carefully ordered. At the top of the pyramid were me and my wife. Then came Gothon Duffé, my valet's lover.

RM: Your valet – La Jeunesse?

MDS: Yes. He left his family to be with Gothon for her enormous ass. Then we had Jean and Saint-Louis, a drunk. He was a terror, feared no one. Nanon was the housekeeper. Then we had my young male secretary, who was about fifteen, and five serving damsels – between twelve and fifteen, I think. My wife assembled the superb cast herself. Then we had a couple of dancers and a cook. All told, it was twenty people.

RM: All of whom were immured in the château, unable to escape.

MDS: Nonsense.

RM: What was your role?

MDS: I was the master of ceremonies. I disciplined them, created tableaux vivants, determined partners – without order the thing would have been an ugly mess. I turned the derangement of the senses into a work of art. I even controlled the emissions.

RM: You hurt the children under your care?

MDS: A great deal of pleasure was had in those two months.

RM: Until one of the little abused girls escaped to her parents and scandal erupted.

MDS: That child was a real hysteric.

RM: How much was your wife involved in the theater of lust you created? I must know – did Renée-Pélagie participate? Were you a sort of crime power couple? Did your wife, that meek, plain, dumpy woman – did she or did she not indulge in your sadistic pranks?

MDS: Renée-Pélagie was the steward of my fantasies. She was my angel. I raised her above other women. Above the law. She and I were like demigods for a time.

RM: But did she participate?

MDS: Why are you so obsessed with sex? I honor my wife – our intimate life is not for observation. But no, in answer to your sordid question.

RM: Where I come from, you are a famous writer. You have become a symbol of personal freedom for some, of monstrous excess for others. We can't get enough of you.

MDS: Are you Swedish? Are they performing my plays in Sweden and I don't know it?

RM: Your plays ... no, I'm afraid they are forgotten. The books are remembered: *Philosophy in the Bedroom, Justine, The 120 Days of Sodom*.

MDS: How is this possible? The manuscript for *The 120 Days of Sodom* is ...

RM: ... hidden in a chest in your prison cell.

MDS: I don't know what you are talking about. What are *Philosophy in the Bedroom* and *Justine*?

RM: Oh. Sorry. You haven't written those yet.

MDS: You are obviously a lunatic.

RM: If you had never been imprisoned you might never have become a writer. You would have just organized orgies. Being in prison is perhaps the ideal place for a writer to get any work done.

MDS: How delightful are the pleasures of the imagination! In these delectable moments, the whole world is ours. Not a single creature resists us, we devastate the world, we repopulate it with new objects, which, in turn, we immolate. The means to every crime is ours, and we employ them all, we multiply them a hundredfold.

RM: Well, the crimes of your body and your imagination have earned you an adjective out here. And noun! *Sadism. Sadistic.* Meaning 'taking pleasure in cruelty'.

MDS: They boiled me down to *that*!

RM: For the most part.

MDS: I am a man of the theater. I . . . staged things.

RM: But in so doing you sometimes tied children up and beat them.

MDS: My godfather used to shoot workers off of rooftops, and he got pardoned by the King. But when I paddle a prostitute, I am penalized.

RM: According to Inspector Buhot, when you were twenty-eight, you locked a woman in a room, threatened her with a knife until she beat you, then you masturbated with a crucifix and forced her to do the same. Even by the standards of libertinage, that's pretty extreme.

MDS: She was a prostitute! And she never pressed charges.

RM: All that desecration, though. For an atheist, you seem very angry at a God you don't believe in.

MDS: The invention of God is the one thing I truly cannot forgive man for.

RM: Why?

MDS: I imagine the Last Judgement this way: God will upbraid the good. He will say, 'When you saw everything was vicious and criminal on earth, why did you stray into the path of virtue? Did not the perpetual misery with which I covered the universe suffice to convince you that I love only disorder and chaos, and that to please me you must irritate me? Did I not daily provide you with the example of destruction? Seeing which, fools, why did you not destroy? Why did you not do as I did?'

RM: So you believe in God – but not a merciful God?

MDS: It is in the name of Nature that I wage war against God and morality.

RM: But your tastes are unnatural. Your cruelty is unnecessary. Nature is dictated by necessity.

MDS: It's true, my desire to desecrate Nature is stronger than my need to offend God. I would like to upset her plans, arrest the wheeling courses of the stars, destroy what serves Nature and protect what is harmful to her . . . and this I am unable to do.

RM: You would be a god.

MDS: I would be a completely free human being. That is all.

RM: The personal freedom you describe leaves no room for a social contract. For ethics. For social responsibility.

MDS: Oh, please. There is no possible comparison between what others experience and what we sense. The heaviest dose of agony in others means nothing to us, yet the tiniest dose of pleasure, registered in us, does touch us deeply.

RM: It makes me think of disasters on the news – or accidents on the road. They elicit curiosity more than compassion . . .

MDS: The source of all our moral errors lies in the ridiculous fiction of brotherhood the Christians invented. The truth is we are all born enemies, all in a state of perpetual and reciprocal warfare.

RM: That's depressing.

MDS: What is depressing is the lies the Christians came up with.

RM: This freedom you speak of. It's only for men, I suppose?

MDS: In the future as I imagine it, there will be houses of libertinage for women, under the government's protection. In these establishments there will be all the individuals of either sex a woman could desire.

RM: Really?

MDS: O charming sex, you will be free! Women have been endowed with considerably more violent penchants for carnal pleasure than we. In my ideal society they would be allowed to give themselves over to it, absolutely free of all encumbering family ties, false notions of modesty – absolutely restored to a state of nature. I want laws permitting women to give themselves to as many men as they see fit. I would also have a law whereby all women must give themselves to whatever man wants her. We owe it to them that they get the same privilege.

RM: So . . . let me get this straight. Women have to give themselves to any man who wants them. But also, they can have any man—

MDS: Or woman—

RM: Any man or woman whom they desire. What about families?

MDS: What can the family matter in the new Republic, where every individual must have no mother but the nation, where everyone born is the motherland's child? Children should be separated from their family and raised by the state. No child must know the identity of his father. All children must be children of their country.

RM: I had no idea how radical you were.

MDS: These are just ideas I am batting about.

RM: Not what you actually believe?

MDS: I believe I need clean linen.

RM: Doesn't your wife send you any?

MDS: Not for weeks.

RM: There's going to be a revolution in France.

MDS: Probably.

RM: No. There is.

MDS: Anarchy?

RM: For a time.

MDS: Finally. The rule of law is inferior to that of anarchy. But then ... no more?

RM: Anarchy, chaos for a time, in France. Then a dictator. A little bourgeois Corsican.

MDS: Oh, God.

RM: Have you ever been in love?

MDS: Many times.

RM: With a man or a woman?

MDS: Women! I succumb happily to men, but I always love the sight of a woman's white bottom, with its little puckered rose beckoning me.

RM: You prefer sodomy even with women?

MDS: Vastly. The vagina is the ultimate cul-de-sac. If you are timid enough to stop with what is natural, Nature will elude your grasp for ever.

RM: Do you love to be hurt as you love to hurt?

MDS: I take pleasure in being whipped and in whipping. But there is no slavishness or shame in my liking for degradation. For a mind as organized as mine, that humiliation serves as an exquisite flattery to my pride.

RM: What do you crave above all things?

MDS: Right now? A roast chicken.

Ian Rankin

interviews

ARTHUR CONAN DOYLE

IAN RANKIN, *author of the Inspector Rebus series, was born in Scotland in 1960.*

ARTHUR CONAN DOYLE, *a Scottish physician and the creator of Sherlock Holmes, died in 1930.*

ARTHUR CONAN DOYLE: What's happening? What am I doing here?

IAN RANKIN: Amazing what you can do with a Ouija board and a bit of channelling, Sir Arthur.

ACD: Wait, I recognize this place. Calton Hill, is it not?

IR: I brought you here so you could get a panoramic view of the city of your birth. I notice you've still got the accent, too.

ACD: I was brought up in Edinburgh. I attended university here. Who are you?

IR: I'm a novelist, same as you. I write about a detective. In fact, one of the things I wanted to talk to you about was the similarity between us.

ACD: What's that monstrosity down yonder?

IR: Next to the Palace of Holyrood? That's the Scottish Parliament.

ACD: You mean Scotland has broken from England?

IR: Not exactly. I forgot – you're a Unionist, aren't you? Ran for Parliament in Edinburgh a couple of times.

ACD: I did.

IR: Unsuccessfully.

ACD: Must we dwell on that? Are you an Edinburgh man?

IR: Only latterly. Like you, I was brought up working class, but north of here. I came to Edinburgh as a student. I'd started writing.

ACD: As did I. As a child I wrote and illustrated my own stories.

IR: Yeah, same here. Only my first full-length novel had to wait till I was a student here.

ACD: You tasted early success, then?

IR: Not exactly. You, on the other hand?

ACD: I wrote some stories in my late teens and early twenties. I took time out from my medical studies—

IR: To work as a doctor on a whaling ship, right?

ACD: That is correct. We sailed to the Arctic. It was a formative experience.

IR: Me, all I had was a holiday job in a chicken factory. Your first Sherlock Holmes story had trouble finding a home, didn't it?

ACD: I learned the art of perseverance, sir. A novel of mine was lost in the post, yet I continued to write.

IR: I never had that happen. But, like you, I couldn't afford to make copies of my early stuff. My first novel, all there is of it is the manuscript. It was turned down eight or nine times. But the thing I'm interested in, of course, is Holmes.

ACD (*sighing*): Of course. Why should you be different from anyone else?

IR: Wait a second. There is something I need to show you.

Whoooshh . . .

ACD: Where are we now?

IR: Top of Leith Walk. Recognize the statue?

ACD: I assume it is meant to be Holmes.

IR: And look across the street – a pub called the Conan Doyle.

ACD: Edinburgh, it seems, has clutched me to its bosom.

IR: One of the people you studied under, Dr Joseph Bell, he was your template for Holmes, wasn't he?

ACD: Among others. You know the name Vidocq?

IR: Real-life French detective, famous for disguises.

ACD: You are well informed.

IR: But you set your Holmes stories in London rather than Edinburgh or Paris.

ACD: I left Edinburgh as a young man. London was, at that time, more of a criminal city. Only a year after the first Holmes tale, Jack the Ripper began his campaign of terror.

IR: Handy timing on your part.

ACD: I agree. The public were looking for some small comfort. They wanted reassurance that crime was not an intractable problem.

IR: And Holmes gave them that reassurance. I'm assuming that during your time in the hereafter you've discovered the true identity of the Ripper?

ACD: He is not part of my 'hereafter'.

IR: You did a lot of harm, you know.

ACD: In what way?

IR: Your policemen were ill-informed fools and foils, like Inspector Lestrade. For decades afterwards the fictional detective in

England had to be an amateur, a Miss Marple or a Lord Peter Wimsey.

ACD: Holmes was not an amateur.

IR: I know. He was a 'consulting detective', a private eye in other words, which means you also helped create the likes of Marlowe and Sam Spade. And with Watson you created another staple: the faithful sidekick. Do you ever see all those films they've made of your books?

ACD: I have knowledge of them. Basil Rathbone wasn't bad.

IR: I think I prefer *The Seven Per-Cent Solution*. Nicol Williamson plays Holmes and gets to meet Sigmund Freud. But what about Gene Wilder? Or Peter Cook and Dudley Moore?

ACD: Stop, I beg you.

IR: And that's before we get to Spielberg's *Young Sherlock Holmes*, Alan Moore's use of Moriarty and Mycroft in *The League of Extraordinary Gentlemen* and of course Guy Ritchie's big-screen versions with Jude Law and Robert Downey Jr. I even saw a robotic Holmes in a recent *Scooby-Doo* episode.

ACD: No shit, Sherlock, as our American cousins might say.

IR: I see you've not lost your sense of humour. The point I'm making is, you created an icon, a character that can be shaped by and for different generations.

ACD: Do they still read the stories, though?

IR: Some of them do – and dress up in deerstalkers at conventions. There's even a magazine called *Sherlock*. It gives out annual awards.

ACD: From your tone, I deduce that you've won one.

IR: Elementary! I got a Sherlock for Best Detective Created by a
British Author. I want to talk to you about him. See, you got
tired of Holmes, didn't you? Killed him off by sending him
over the Reichenbach Falls.

ACD: You're thinking of dispatching your detective in the same
way?

IR: Not exactly, though I do have a Moriarty figure in my books.
His name is Cafferty and he's the villain who runs Edinburgh.

ACD: Cafferty? Sounds Irish.

IR: I suppose he might be.

ACD: And Catholic?

IR: I forgot you were Catholic yourself.

ACD: I renounced at an early age.

IR: And became a spiritualist. You took part in seances.

ACD: I saw things, the most incredible things.

IR: Ectoplasm, right? Voices telling you things no one but yourself could have known?

ACD: And more.

IR: You didn't manage to convince Harry Houdini. He sat in on a
seance led by your wife, then slated it in a newspaper article.

ACD: He was . . . misguided.

IR: But you could be misguided, too – remember those Bradford
girls, the ones who photographed fairies at the foot of their
garden?

ACD: As with all systems of belief, spiritualism is not free from
frauds and charlatans. And yet you have conjured me here,
meaning you must be a believer in a higher power.

IR: I channel characters all the time. Maybe you're just another one. Come on, let's get a drink. I'm buying.

Whoooshh . . .

ACD: Where are we now?

IR: The Oxford Bar. It's my local. My hero drinks here, too. I'm sorry you're not corporeal enough for a dram.

ACD: But I can smell the malt; that's welcoming enough. You say your hero drinks here?

IR: His name is Rebus. Some people think he has a drink problem. The thing is, he's getting old. I made him forty in the first book and he lives in real time. That makes him fifty-six now, and the cops in Scotland retire at sixty.

ACD: You are facing your own Reichenbach, in a manner of speaking. I'm not sure I can help. Yes, I felt stifled by Holmes. I wanted to write fantasy and serious fiction.

IR: You once said crime fiction was 'a lower stratum of literary achievement'. I know quite a few present-day crime writers who would contest that.

ACD: Hardly my concern, sir. But the lure of money and the heartbreak of my readers conspired to revive Holmes, much as your whisky is reviving my memories of Edinburgh's low drinking dens.

IR: You feel your non-Holmes books are underrated? For what it's worth, some critics now agree with you. It's funny, the last book I finished reading was all about Holmes. It's by Michael

Chabon and imagines your hero in extreme old age, at the time of the Second World War.

ACD: Let's not discuss those wars.

IR: Of course . . . I'm sorry. You lost your son in the First World War.

ACD: Yes.

IR: You visited the trenches, wrote propaganda. Same with the Boer War. You wrote in defence of British tactics there, after working as a surgeon on the battlefield.

ACD: It is important to stand by one's beliefs. People these days don't seem so willing. But to attempt a change of subject – none too subtly, I'm sure you'll agree – have you ever used my work as a template for your own?

IR: Sure. One of Rebus's early sidekicks is called Brian Holmes and I had a police chief called Watson. Then there was 'The Acid Test' . . .

ACD: And what was that?

IR: A short story I wrote a while back. Sorry, but it turned out you were the murderer.

ACD: Was I? By Jove!

IR: You don't sound upset.

ACD: Actually, I have to confess that I've read it. Not much else to do in the hereafter but keep an eye on one's competitors. I know, for example, that you once worked as a music journalist in Upper Norwood. I assume you're aware that I had a home in South Norwood? More connects us than you might think. I also know that your father was a Freemason, as was I, but you've never been persuaded to join. You have campaigned about certain perceived injustices, as did I in my heyday. All this information I could have used to startle you, in the style of Holmes.

IR: But you didn't.

ACD: Because I'm not him. I'm a man who saw life, from whaling ships to serving the national interest in two wars. I knew great men – Hardy, Wilde, Chesterton, Wells. I lost a wife to consumption and a son to enemy action. I saw the world in all its facets.

IR: Do you still see the world? What sort of mess are we in right now?

ACD: I remain an 'optimistic imperialist'. I feel the British Empire exerted a largely positive influence on its colonies.

IR: And is that what the US is doing?

ACD: Ah, politics . . . What an arid discussion that would engender!

IR: You're probably right.

ACD: You know I must leave soon?

IR: You're already fading.

ACD: The other world calls to me. It's a world not all are privileged to see. Do you have a final question for me?

IR: I don't think so . . . No, wait! Here's one. What did you think of Gerry Rafferty's 'Baker Street'? Hey, Sir Arthur! Artie! You still there?

BARMAN: Jesus, Ian, keep the noise down, pal. I think you were on your way.

IR: Fuck off, I've only had one.

B: Ya daft bastard, you've been here all afternoon. And what's
    with the mess on the table – torn bits of beer mat made into
    a circle and the whisky glasses turned upside-down in the
    midst of it all?

IR: I was just . . . Nothing, Harry. Nothing.

Joyce Carol Oates

creates Evangeline Fife, who interviews

ROBERT FROST

Lovely, Dark, Deep

JOYCE CAROL OATES, *an American novelist, poet, critic, professor and editor, was born in 1938.*

ROBERT FROST, *an American poet, died in 1963.*

'EVANGELINE FIFE', *a student, met Frost at the Bread Loaf Writers' Conference, Bread Loaf, Vermont, on 18 August 1951.*

Here was the first surprise: the great man was much heavier, much more *solid-bodied*, than I'd anticipated. You would not have called him *fat* – that would have been insulting, and inaccurate; but his torso sagged against his shirt like a great udder, and his thighs in summer trousers were a middle-aged woman's fleshy thighs. The sensitive-young-poet face of the photos – (at least, the photos I'd affixed to my bedroom wall) – had coarsened and thickened; deep lines now bracketed the eyes, as if the poet had too often scowled, or squinted, or winked to suggest the (secret) wickedness of the words he was uttering. The snowy-white hair so often captured in photographs like ectoplasm lifting from the poet's head was thinner than any photograph had suggested, and not so snowy-white, disheveled as if the poet had only just arisen dazed from sleep. The entire face looked large – larger than you expect a poet's face to be – and the thick jaws were covered in glittering little hairs as if the poet hadn't shaved for a day or two. The eyelids were drooping, near-shut.

'Excuse me – Mr Frost?'

My voice was tentative, apologetic. My heart had begun to beat erratically as some small, perishable creature – butterfly, moth – might beat against its confinement.

For here was the great man – so suddenly. In my nervous excitement I'd anticipated walking much farther along the path to the poet's cabin in the woods – the 'Poet's Cabin' as it was called. I'd anticipated knocking at a door, and waiting for the door to be opened. (Surely not by the legendary Robert Frost himself but by an assistant or secretary? Widowed since 1938, as I'd made it a point to know, the poet would not have been protected by a wary wife, at least.) Instead, Mr Frost was awaiting his interviewer outside the cabin on a small porch, slouched in a swing, seemingly dozing; slack-jawed, and a scribble of saliva on his mouth. In the bunched crotch of his baggy old-man trousers was an opened notebook and on the floor of the plank porch was the poet's pencil.

Mr Frost seemed to have drifted into a trance-like sleep in the midst of writing a poem. I felt a stab of excitement at such unexpected intimacy – *Gazing upon Robert Frost asleep! And no one knows.*

On a table beside the porch swing was a pitcher of what appeared to be lemonade and two glasses, of which one was a quarter-filled; a strangely loud-ticking alarm clock; and a dingy red fly swatter.

Quickly I glanced about: no one appeared to be watching. The receptionist whom I'd met in the Bread Loaf Conference Center at the foot of the drive had sent me unaccompanied to Mr Frost – 'You're expected, Miss Fife. Just go on up to the Poet's Cabin. And remember, you must not stay more than an hour, even if Mr Frost is generous with his time and invites you.'

Primly this middle-aged woman smiled at me, and primly Evangeline Fife smiled back. *Of course! Certainly, ma'am.*

The Bread Loaf Writers' Conference, as it was called, was a very busy place at this time of year; there were hundreds of visiting writers, poets and students of all ages (with a preponderance of well-to-do middle-aged women). But this part of the grounds, behind the administrative offices and the white clapboard residences of the chief administrators, was cordoned off as *Private*.

Like an earnest schoolgirl, I was carrying a large straw satchel weighted down with books, tape recorder, notebook, wallet. Out of this straw satchel came, now, quick into my hands, my newly purchased Kodak Hawkeye.

For it seemed that Mr Frost hadn't heard my faltering voice – hadn't opened his eyes. In my shaky hands I positioned the camera – peered through the viewfinder at the shadowy figure within with its ghostly-white hair – dared to press the shutter. Very carefully then I wound the film to the next picture.

Like stopping to reload a shotgun, such photography was. You did not simply 'take pictures' in rapid succession – each act of picture-taking was deliberate and premeditated.

How strangely vulnerable Mr Frost looked to me, like an older relative, a father, a grandfather, whom you might glimpse lying about the house carelessly groomed and only partly dressed; it was said that the poet was vain of his appearance, and insisted upon exerting veto power over most photographs of himself, and so it was by chance I'd come upon him in this slovenly state between sleep and wakefulness, as in a hypnotic trance. On his bare feet, well-worn leather house slippers.

I smiled to think *Maybe he is dreaming of – an interview? An interviewer who has come to him, in stealth?*

In all, I took seven surreptitious pictures that afternoon of Mr Frost slack-jawed and dozing on a porch swing. Sold to a private collector, resold to another collector, and one day to be placed in the Robert Frost Special Collections in the Middlebury College Library, discreetly catalogued *Bread Loaf August 1951 (photographer unknown).*

Taking Mr Frost's picture without permission was a brazen act, I know. I had never done anything remotely like this before in my life – at least, I didn't recall having done anything like this: appropriated something not mine, that I believed to be mine; that I believed I *deserved*. Yet all this while I was trembling in dread of Mr Frost waking and discovering me. Exhilaration coursed through my body like a swift, sexual shock – *I will steal the poet's soul! It is what I deserve.*

It was in the late summer of 1951, when I was thirty-one years old and a candidate for a master's degree in English at Middlebury College, that I drove to the Bread Loaf Writers' Conference to interview Robert Frost for a special issue of *Poetry Parnassus.*

At this time, Evangeline Fife was a promising poet as well as an English instructor at the Privet Academy for Girls in Marblehood, Massachusetts, from which I'd graduated in 1938; since fall of 1950, I'd been accepted into the rigorous master's program at Middlebury College. It was my hope to advance myself in some way, if only by improving my teaching credentials that I might apply for a position at a four-year college or university. (Of course, it was clear to me that few women were hired for such positions, except at women's colleges; and even there, men were favored. Still, I wished to think that I'd been encouraged by my professors in the Middlebury program; for I'd published poetry in several well-regarded literary magazines including *Poetry Parnassus*, whose editors I'd convinced to empower me to interview the seventy-seven-year-old Robert Frost.) My thesis advisor at Middlebury happened to be, not entirely coincidentally, the director of the summer Bread Loaf Writers' Conference, and he'd encouraged me in both my poetry and my academic studies; kindly Professor Diggs had intervened on my behalf with the famous poet, who declined most requests for interviews – at least interviews with 'unknown' parties and for little-known publications like *Poetry Parnassus*.

I was conscious of the great honor of being allowed to interview Robert Frost, the preeminent American poet of the era, and I prepared with more than my usual assiduousness. This meant reading, and rereading, virtually all of Frost's poems, many of which, without having intended to, I'd memorized as a schoolgirl. As early as middle school my grandmother had read to me such Frost poems as 'The Road Not Taken', 'The Death of the Hired Man', 'Birches', 'Mending Wall' and (Grandmother's personal favorite) 'Stopping by Woods'. My English instructors at the

Privet Academy had reinforced my admiration for Frost, and for poetry in general; at Berkshire College for Women, I majored in English, and published poetry in *Berkshire Blossoms*, which I edited in my senior year. As a junior instructor in English at Privet, I taught Robert Frost's poetry alongside the poetry of Shelley, Keats, Wordsworth and Byron. Of course, I'd heard Mr Frost read his poetry several times in Massachusetts and Vermont, always to large, rapturous and uncritical audiences. The atmosphere at these celebrated readings was reverential yet festive, for Robert Frost had become known as a Yankee sage who was also a Yankee wit – a 'homespun' American who was also a seer.

Are you wondering what I looked like? No observer would have been surprised to learn that Evangeline Fife was a 'poetess' – (as women poets were known at this time) – but it should certainly be noted that I was a pretty – *quite pretty* – young woman who'd always looked younger than her age, which is, for women, the most satisfying sort of deception.

A man might enjoy being mistaken for being more sexually aggressive than he is, and richer. But for women, age is paramount.

It is true, I was not a strikingly beautiful woman, which would have involved an entirely different sort of strategy in confronting the (male) world – one far more cautious and circuitous – but my sort of wan delicate blond prettiness seemed preferable than beauty to many men. The *striking beauty* is the female a man can't control in the way he might imagine he could control the delicately blond *merely pretty* woman who at thirty-one can still pass for a girl of eighteen.

Also, I was *petite*. Men imagine that they can more readily intimidate a *petite* female.

Evangeline Fife was not married, nor even engaged. This you would note immediately by glancing at the third finger of her left hand – which was bare. Like most girls and young women of her sort, of the era, Miss Fife was certainly a *virgin*.

By *virgin* is meant not simply, or merely, a physiological state but a spiritual state as well. *Pure, innocent, unsullied, artless* – these were adjectives that might have described me, and would have been flattering to me, as to any young unmarried girl of the time.

Though at thirty-one, and still unmarried, Evangeline Fife wasn't exactly *young* any longer, I hoped that Mr Frost, at seventy-seven, would see me differently.

'Excuse me, Mr Frost? I am – Evangeline Fife? I have a – an appointment with you at one o'clock . . .'

Thrillingly my voice quavered. If you'd placed your forefinger against my throat, as the dozing poet might have been imagining he did, you would feel a sensuous vibratory hum.

The elderly poet's eyelids fluttered and blinked open. For a startled moment Mr Frost didn't seem to know where he was – outside? On a porch swing? *Had he been sleeping? And what time was this?*

His first, fearful glance was at the alarm clock on the table beside the swing. From where I stood, I could not see the clock-face clearly but had an impression that the glass was glaring with reflected light. The clock was of slightly larger than ordinary size, trimmed in brass, with a look of a nautical instrument; its ticking was unusually loud, and seemed quickened.

The poet then saw me – blinking again, and even rubbing at his eyes. Ah, an attractive young stranger! – standing some ten feet in front of him in the grass, with fine-brushed pale-blond hair and widened 'periwinkle-blue' worshipful eyes like a poetry-loving schoolgirl. As a portly peacock might do, quickly the poet took measure of himself, glancing down at his bulky body. His large hands lifted to pat down his disheveled hair, stroke his unshaven jaws, adjust his shirt where it swelled over his belt buckle. He frowned at me, and smiled, as a cunning look came into the faded-icy-blue eyes, and there emerged as through parted curtains on a brightly lit stage the New England sage 'Robert Frost' of the famed poetry readings.

'Yes! Of course. I've been awaiting you, my dear. You are prompt – one o'clock. But I am *prompter*, you see, for I am already *here*.'

Unfortunately the notebook precariously balanced in the poet's lap fell to the ground. Clumsy, flummoxed and sensing himself not so nimble, Mr Frost seemed disinclined to stoop over and pick up the notebook – so, with a little curtsy, I did.

(It was an ordinary spiral notebook, with a black marbleized cover. What I could see of the pages, they were covered in pencil scrawls.)

Mr Frost seemed embarrassed, taking the notebook from my fingers. 'Thank you, my dear.'

Very like a schoolgirl I stood before the poet whose gaze

moved up and down my body with the finesse of a practiced gem-appraiser. It is always an anxious moment before a woman understands the male judgment – *Yes! You will do.*

(After much deliberation that morning, before setting off on my pilgrimage, I'd selected a pink floral-print cotton 'shirtwaist' with a flared skirt that fell below the knee. On my slender feet were black patent-leather 'ballerina flats'. My pale-blond hair was brushed and gleaming and tied back with a pink velvet ribbon. Of course, the Kodak Hawkeye had vanished into my straw bag as if it had never been.)

Mr Frost was murmuring what a lovely surprise this was, that the interviewer for *Poetry* was – *me.*

'So often the interviewer is beetle-browed and grim – if a young man; and thick-waisted and plain as suet – if female.' The poet chuckled mischievously, rubbing his hands together.

There was the *Yankee sage.* Yet more beloved, the *mischievous Yankee sage.*

A blush rose into my face. Being so complimented, at the expense of other, less fortunate interviewers, was an ambiguous gift: to accept would be vain, to seem to decline would be rude. A young female soon learns the *slitheringness* of accommodation to her (male) elders, by a faint frown of a smile.

Yet I had no choice but to murmur an apology: 'Except, Mr Frost, it isn't *Poetry* – but *Poetry Parnassus.*'

Mr Frost grunted, he wasn't sure he'd heard of *Poetry Parnassus.*

'You will be featured on the cover, Mr Frost. As I explained in my letter.'

Still, Mr Frost frowned. A sort of thundery malevolence gathered in his brow.

Quickly I said, 'I mean – the entire October issue will be devoted to "Robert Frost".'

This placated the poet, to a degree. He'd recovered something of his composure, placing the notebook on the table beside the swing, and taking up, in a playful manner, the red plastic fly swatter.

'And what did you say your name is, dear?'

'My name is – Evangeline Fife.'

Mr Frost gazed at me with mirthful eyes. '"Evangeline Fife" – a truly inspired name. Is it authentic, or shrewdly invented on the spot to prick the poet's curiosity?'

What a strange question! My thin-skinned face, already blushing, grew warmer still. My reply was a stammer: 'I – I am – my name is "authentic", Mr Frost.'

'As authentic as "Robert Frost", eh?'

This was very clever! Or so it seemed to me. For *Robert Frost* was the ideal name for the individual who'd created the poetry of *Robert Frost*.

'Please have a seat, dear Miss Fife. Forgive an old man's rudeness, for not rising with alacrity at your approach . . .'

Mr Frost made a courteous little gesture, simulating the action of rising to his feet without actually moving, and extending a hand to me in a gentlemanly manner, though it was imperative for me to come to *him*, to allow my hand to be gripped in his plump-dimpled hand, and shaken briskly.

With a little grunt Mr Frost tugged me up onto the porch to sit beside him on the swing – but discreetly I took another seat in a rattan chair.

'I think, my dear, the cushion on that chair is damp.'

Belatedly, I realized that this was so. But I only just laughed airily and insisted that the chair was fine, for I did not wish to sit close beside the elderly poet on the swing.

Mr Frost was slapping the fly swatter lightly against his knee. 'If it becomes too damp, my dear, please tell me – we'll find another place for your – for you.'

With mock primness the poet smiled. Wanting me to understand how he'd refrained from saying *for your tender little bottom*.

Embarrassed, I was about to turn on my tape recorder and ask my first question, when, as if he'd only now thought of it, Mr Frost said, 'And who are the "Fifes", my dear?'

My heart sank in dismay. I'd never thought of my family and relatives as *the Fifes* – it was rare that I gave them much thought at all.

The poet's faded-icy-blue gaze seemed to be pressing against my chest. I could not breathe easily. I managed to stammer a weak reply: 'My family and my father's relatives live in Maine, mostly in Bangor.'

'Bangor! Not a hospitable place for the cultivation of poetry, I think.' Mr Frost smiled at me, tapping the fly swatter lightly on his knee. 'And your mother's relatives, Miss Fife?'

'She – they – there were ancestors who'd lived in Salem, Massachusetts . . .'

Gleefully Mr Frost said, 'Ah, there's a history, my dear! Were your mother's Salem ancestors *witch-hunters*, or *witches*?'

'I – I don't think so, Mr Frost . . .'

'If you don't know with certainty, it's likely that your ancestors were *witches*. The *witch-hunters* were the ruling class of the Puritan settlements, and no one is ashamed of being descended from any ruling class.'

None of this made sense to me, entirely. Mr Frost chuckled at my look of incomprehension. It would seem to have been an old, much-loved ploy of the poet's – confounding an interviewer with questions of his own.

He'd folded his large hands over his belly, which strained the white cotton shirt above his belt. I had a glimpse of the elderly poet's exposed navel, a spiraling little vortex of hairs around a miniature knob of flesh quaint as a mummified snail. Like a New England Buddha the poet reclined, a figure of complacent (male) wisdom.

Even as I asked Mr Frost if we might begin our interview, he said, ignoring me, slapping the fly swatter against the palm of a hand, '"Thou shalt not suffer a witch to live" – the Americans understand this admonition, deep in their killer-souls. All that remains for our fellow citizens is to locate the "witch" among us – for that, like the most vicious hunting dogs, they require guidance.' Mr Frost smiled with a strange sort of satisfaction. '"I have a lover's quarrel with the world" – but I would not really like it if the "world" had any sort of quarrel with me.'

In the way of a bull who is both rambling and aggressive,

prone to whimsical turns the observer can't predict, Mr Frost reminisced at length on the subject of witch-hunting and witches and the 'witchery' of the poet, for poetry must always be 'a kind of code'; by this time I'd switched the tape recorder on, and had began to take shorthand in my notebook as well, for I did not want to lose a single, precious syllable of Mr Frost's. I thought of Frost's bizarre poem 'The Witch of Coos' – the bones of a long-ago murder victim hiking up the cellar steps of a remote old farmhouse in New Hampshire, nailed behind the headboard of a marital bed in an attic – like an ancient curse stirring to life. If the poet had written only this singular poem – along with one or two other poems spoken by deranged New England narrators – the reputation of Robert Frost would be that of a master of *gothic*.

'Do *you* believe in witches, Mr Frost?'

It was the bold desperation of the timid, such an awkward query, made when Mr Frost paused for breath; and met with a disdainful frown such as an impertinent child might receive from an elder. With a sneering smile Mr Frost said, 'Poetry isn't in the business of *believing*, Miss Fife. *Believing* is a crudeness that is the prerogative of other, lesser beings.'

These words were a sort of rebuff to my naïveté but I was eager to transcribe the startling aphorism, which was entirely new to me. If Robert Frost had uttered it previously, or committed it to writing, I was unaware of it.

Poetry . . . not in the business of believing.

Believing . . . a crudeness the prerogative of other, lesser beings.

(Very different from the 'homespun' Frost so beloved by people like my grandmother!)

As Mr Frost spoke, his faded-icy-blue eyes darted shrewdly about, and with sudden alacrity he wielded the fly swatter – crushing a large fly that had come to rest on a porch post nearby. The black, broken body fell into the grass.

'If only the ignorant "poetry-haters" among us could be dealt with so readily!' – Mr Frost chuckled.

I was about to ask Mr Frost if he felt that there were 'poetry-haters' in the world, and who these individuals might be; I'd prepared to ask him about Shelley's bold remark that poets are the *unacknowledged legislators* of the world, but had not a chance to speak for Mr Frost then reverted, with the air of an elder teasing a captive child, to the previous subject of *the Fifes* – as if he were suspicious of my identity, or pretending to be so. Asking me when *the Fifes* had emigrated to the United States, and from where, so that I told him that, so far as I knew, *the Fifes* had come to America in the 1880s, from somewhere in Scotland.

Mr Frost seemed just slightly disappointed. 'Ah well – so "your Fifes" are not guilty of persecuting witches, at least not in the New World! And "your Fifes" obviously were not slave owners, nor did they profit from the robust slave trade of pre-Civil War United States – as so many did, whose descendants are canny enough to change the subject when it comes up.'

'Yes, sir. I mean – no. They did not.'

'And where in Scotland did they come from, Miss Fife?'

My tongue felt clumsy in my mouth. For my mouth was very dry.

The poet's perusal of me, the fixedness of his gaze, was making me feel very self-conscious; for it seemed to me that this was the way he'd been looking at the flies that buzzed obliviously about beyond his reach to swat.

'I think – Perth, Inverness . . .'

Sharply Mr Frost said, 'Indeed! But not Leith?'

I had not dared claim this port of Edinburgh, for I knew that Frost's mother had been born there.

'No, sir.'

'But have you visited Scotland, Miss Fife? Are you any sort of "Scots lass"?' The poet's mouth twisted in a smiling sneer with the words *Scots lass*.

I told Mr Frost that I was no sort of 'Scots lass', I was afraid, and that there wasn't money for that sort of lavish travel in my family.

'Ah, a rebuke! Let me assure you, dear, there wasn't money for anything like that in *the Frost family*, either. We were all – very – as my poems indicate – *very poor*, and *very frugal*.' But Mr Frost was laughing kindly, seeing the abashed expression in my face. 'D'you like the verse of Bobbie Burns? "O my Luve's like a red, red rose,/ That's newly sprung in June:/ O, my Luve's like the melodie,/ That's sweetly play'd in tune."' Mr Frost recited the lines with exaggerated rhythm, sneering. 'Gives doggerel a bad name, eh? All dogs might sue.'

Feebly I laughed at this joke. If it was a joke.

A bully is one who forces you to laugh at his jokes, even if they are not jokes. That is how you know he is a bully.

A knitted look came onto the poet's forehead. The mocking eyes relented. 'Though I will have to concede, Burns has written some decent verse, or rather – lines. "Ev'n you on murd'ring errands toil'd,/ Lone from your savage homes exil'd . . ." The man *felt strongly*, which is the beginning of poetry.'

(A ripple of panic came over me: at this rate we would never get to the poet's life, still less to the substance of the interview which was the poetry of Robert Frost. This the man seemed to be hiding behind his back as one might tease a child with a treat the child knows is behind the back, and out of reach.)

Daringly I decided to counter with a question of my own: 'And where are your people from, Mr Frost?'

But this was a blunder, for Mr Frost did not like such contrary motions. Coldly he said, 'That sort of elementary "biographical information" you should already know, Miss Fife. In fact, you should have memorized it. I hope you've done some homework in your subject and don't expect the poor subject to provide information that is publicly available.'

But for a moment I could not speak. I thought *He will send me away. He will laugh at me, and send me away.*

'Oh, Mr Frost, I'm sorry – yes, I do know that you were born in San Francisco, and not in New England – as most people think. And your background isn't rural – you lived in San Francisco until you were eleven, your father was a newspaperman—'

Irritably Mr Frost said, 'That is but *literally true*. In fact I have a considerable "rural background" – I was brought back east by my mother after my father's untimely death and soon – soon I was farming – my paternal grandfather's farm in Derry, New Hampshire. It was clear from the start that "Rob Frost" was a natural man of the soil . . . a New Englander by nature if not actual birth.'

Shutting his eyes, leaning back to make the swing creak, Mr Frost began to recite poems from *A Boy's Will* and *North of Boston*, with perfect recall. These were: 'Mending Wall', 'The Wood-Pile', 'After Apple-Picking' . . .

██ *

The poet spoke in a soft, wondering, lyric voice. There was great beauty in this voice. The New England drawl with its spiteful humor had quite vanished. Now, it was possible to discern the young Robert Frost in the flaccid and creased face – the young poet who'd resembled William Butler Yeats and Rupert Brooke in his dreamy male beauty.

The poet ceased abruptly as if he'd only just realized what this final line from 'After Apple-Picking' meant.

Quickly I asked, 'What does that line mean, Mr Frost? "I am overtired . . ."'

'A poem's "meaning" resides in what it says, Miss Fife.'

* It is long and hallowed a tradition that works of prose and poetry are 'copyright' in the names of writers: this is only sensible. ████████████████ ██ ██ ██ ██ ██ ██ and so we have (sensibly) decided to simply black out the lines in 'copyright'. Inquisitive readers may wish to peruse the relevant poems in *Collected Poems, Prose and Plays*, edited by Mark Richardson and Richard Poirier, Library of America, 1995.

The poet cast a look in my direction that, had it been a swat from the dingy red fly swatter, would have struck me flat in the face. As it was, I couldn't help recoiling, just perceptibly.

Frost's second book, *North of Boston*, contained another of his early masterpieces, 'Home Burial'. This poem, the poet never read to audiences. I asked him if the 'man' and the 'woman' in the poet were himself and his wife, Elinor, at the time of their first son's death, in 1899, at the age of three; a death that might have been prevented except for the mother's Christian Science beliefs. I quoted the powerful line of the woman: '█████████ █████████████████████'

Mr Frost stared at me for a long moment, with something like hatred. His eyes were narrowed, his face contorted in stubbornness. There was no mistaking the man for the kindly New England bard. But he did not answer my question. As if this were an issue that had to be set right, he reverted to his previous subject: 'Only a poet who knew rural life intimately could have written any of my "country" poems. There is no other poetry quite like them, in American poetry. In England, perhaps the poetry of John Clare, and Wordsworth – but these are very different, obviously.'

'Yes, sir. Very different.'

'You see that, do you? Miss Fife?'

'Yes, sir. I think so . . .'

Mr Frost tossed the fly swatter onto the table and was rubbing his large hands. I thought how curious, the backs of his hands were creased and elderly, but the palms smooth. A sly light came into the faded eyes. 'I am wondering, Miss Fife—'

'Please call me Evangeline, sir.'

'But you must not call me Rob, you know. That would not be right.'

'Mr Frost, yes. I would not presume.'

'I have been wondering, *Evangeline* – are you comfortable in that chair?'

I was not so comfortable. But quickly I smiled *yes*.

'You've not become just slightly – damp?'

My bottom was in fact damp, for the cushion was damp and had eked through the skirt of my dress, my silk slip and my cotton panties. But I did not care to betray my discomfort.

'Your bottom, dear? Your delightful little bottom? Your white cotton panties – are they damp?'

I hesitated, stunned. I had no idea how to respond to the poet's teasing query.

So shocked! My notebook nearly slipped from my fingers.

Seeing that he'd so discomfited his interviewer, Mr Frost laughed heartily. He apologized, though not very sincerely: 'I'm very sorry, my dear. My late wife chastised me for my "coarse barnyard" humor. *She* was very sensitive – of course. But there are females drawn to such humor, I believe.'

Mr Frost paused, gazing at me. The faded-blue eyes moved along my (bare) slender legs another time to my (bare) slender ankles, lifted again to my legs, my (imagined) thighs inside the flaring skirt, and the cloth-covered belt cinching my small waist so tight, a man might fantasize closing his large hands about it.

'You might want to change your panties, Evangeline. And take another seat here on the porch, one without a damp cushion.' Again Mr Frost patted the swing seat close beside him, and again I pretended not to notice.

I knew that Mr Frost was teasing me. Yet, I had no other recourse than to say, with a blush, that I couldn't 'change' my panties since I didn't have another, dry pair to put on.

'Really, my dear! You came to Bread Loaf to interview the revered Mr Frost, with but a single pair of panties.' Mr Frost laughed heartily, seeing how embarrassed I was. 'Risky, my dear. Reckless. For you must know that the notorious womanizer Untermeyer is on the premises – and the young, dashing John Ciardi.' Mr Frost peered at me, to see how I interpreted this ambiguous remark. (Of course, I had heard of Louis Untermeyer and John Ciardi, who were both poet-friends and supporters of Robert Frost; the poet was fiercely loyal to his friends, as he was said to be fiercely loyal as an enemy.) 'And you are a poet – poetess? – yourself, I believe.' Mr Frost lay back against the porch swing at an awkward angle, as if inviting another to lie back with him; the old swing creaked faintly. His fingers were stretched over his belly as over a ribald little drum. 'Or is it the lack of foresight of an innocent virgin?' The words *innocent virgin* were lightly stressed.

Seeing that his coarse jesting was meeting with a blank expression in his wanly blond young-woman interviewer, Mr Frost sighed, in an exaggerated sort of disappointment, and may have rolled his eyes to an invisible audience that reacted with near-audible laughter. With a wink he said, 'Well! You must be the judge, dear girl, of the degree of dampness of your panties. No one else can make that decision, I quite agree.'

Panties! What did the great man care about *panties!* I'd resolved to ignore these lewd remarks, as they were unworthy of a poet of such distinction; though, of course, my tape recorder was recording everything Mr Frost said.

My notebook was opened to the first page of questions, carefully transcribed in my neat schoolgirl hand, and numbered; but before I could begin, the mischievous old man peered at me again and said, 'You are a "good" girl, it seems, Evangeline! I should hope so. And what blue eyes! Of the hue of the New England "heal-all" – has anyone ever told you?'

Did Mr Frost expect me not to know to which of his famous poems he was alluding? Shyly I said, 'Except if the heal-all is *white*, Mr Frost.'

'Eh! You are quite correct, my dear.'

The oblique flirtatiousness of the *virgin poetess* had taken Mr Frost somewhat by surprise.

An ideal opportunity! The poet was gazing at me as if hoping to be surprised further. And so in my low, thrilled, vibratory voice I recited 'Design':

Mr Frost laughed and took up the fly swatter, striking the porch railing in applause. He couldn't have been more delighted if a small child had recited his poem without the slightest idea of its meaning.

'That is my most wicked sonnet, my dear. I'm frankly surprised you would have memorized it.'

I responded that 'Design' was a perfectly executed Petrarchan sonnet which I'd memorized as a schoolgirl years ago – 'before I understood it'.

'And d'you feel that you understand it now, dear Evangeline?'

You little fool, trained in poetry by spinster schoolteachers, what do you know of me?

I was reluctant to take up this challenge. In my dampened undergarments I sat with meek-lowered eyes, turning over a page of my notebook, while on the table the alarm clock continued its relentless *tick, tick-tock, tick-tick-tock* – that would have been distracting except for the intensity of our conversation.

In a more serious tone Mr Frost said, 'In great poetry there is always something "signatory" – a word, a phrase, a break in rhythm, a stanza break – that is unexpected. No ordinary versifier could come up with it. In Emily Dickinson's work, virtually every poem contains the "signatory" element. In Robert Frost's work, it's to be hoped that many poems do. For you see, my dear, in reciting the poem, you blundered with one word – "wayside". Instead, you recalled the more commonplace "roadside".'

Was this so? I tried to recall, confused. *Roadside, wayside?*

The poet said, more kindly than chiding, 'If you can't sense the difference between the two words, you are not sensitive to the higher calculus of poetry.'

'Mr Frost, I'm sorry! It was a silly mistake.'

'It was not a *silly mistake*, but a mistake of the sort most people would naturally make, trying to recall a "perfect" poem. Of course, *you* could not recall, my dear Evangeline, because *you* could not have written the poem. As *you* could not emulate the conditions that give rise to the poem, originally: "a lump in the throat, a sense of wrong, a homesickness, a lovesickness".'

The poet seemed satisfied, now. Mr Frost was the sort of bully, very familiar to girls and women, who is fond of his victim even as he is contemptuous of her; whose fondness for her may be an expression of his contempt, like his teasing. He lay back in the swing, fingers folded over the Buddha-belly.

The sun was shifting in the sky: now, the afternoon had begun to wane. Overhead, a *soughing* in the treetops.

Half-consciously I'd been smelling something both sweet

and mildly astringent – a smell of fresh-cut grass. There came to me a blurred memory of childhood, like frost on a window-pane through which you can see only the outline of a figure, or a shadow. The poet is the emissary to childhood, and all things lost. I thought *He is not a wicked man, that he can lead us there. If only he would not misuse his power.*

The *ticking* of the wind-up clock merged with cries of crickets in the tall grasses at the edge of the clearing. Uncertain what I should do, I glanced through my notebook pages, as Mr Frost sighed, and stirred. He opened a single eye, and regarded me quizzically: 'In your printed piece, I suppose you will mention the alarm clock, dear Evangeline? It's because I hate watches, you see. Wearing a watch, as fools do, is like wearing a badge of your own mortality.'

These mordant words, I recorded in my notebook.

'The poem is always about "mortality", you see. The poem is the poet's mainstay against death.'

In the trees overhead, that *soughing* sound that is both pleasur-able and discomfiting, like a memory to which emotion accrues. Except we have forgotten the emotion.

Belatedly Mr Frost offered me a glass of lemonade, which I poured for myself, as I replenished the poet's glass as well; for Mr Frost was one of those men who seem incapable of lifting a hand to serve themselves, still less others. This, I didn't at all mind doing, of course, for I'd been trained to serve, especially my influ-ential elders.

I took a small sip of the lukewarm, oversweet lemonade. My mouth was very dry.

I resumed the interview with a friendly, familiar sort of question: 'Mr Frost, will you tell the readers of *Poetry Parnassus* what you hope to convey in your poetry?'

Mr Frost laughed derisively. 'If I "hoped to convey" something, Miss Fife, I would send a telegram.'

Very good! I laughed, and wrote this down.

In my schoolgirl fashion I went through a list of questions aimed to draw from the poet quotable quotes, which would be valuable to the readers of *Poetry Parnassus*, virtually all of them poets themselves. Pleasurably, Mr Frost leaned back, his hands locked behind his neck, stretched and yawned and answered my questions in his New England drawl, which was both self-mocking and serious. Countless times the great poet had been interviewed; countless times he'd answered these very questions, which he'd memorized, as he had memorized his carefully thought-out replies. Unlike other poets who would have become restless, irritable and bored being asked familiar questions, Mr Frost seemed to bask in the familiarity, indeed like a Buddha who never tires of being worshipped. How different this slack-faced old man was from the dreamy-eyed poet in his early twenties, on my bedroom wall! Long ago he'd composed his aphoristic replies, worn smooth now as much-handled stones. *Free verse* – 'Playing tennis without a net'. *Poetry* – 'A momentary stay against confusion'. *Lyric poetry* – 'Ice melting on a hot stove'. *Love* – 'An irresistible desire to be irresistibly desired'. *On invitations to poetry 'festivals'* – 'If I'm not the show, I don't go.' *Opinion of rival Amy Lowell* – 'A fake'. *Opinion of rival T. S. Eliot* – 'A fake'. *Opinion of rival Ezra Pound* – 'A fake'.

Opinion of rival Archibald MacLeish – 'A fake'. *Opinion of rival Wallace Stevens* – 'Bric-a-brac fake!' *Opinion of rival Carl Sandburg* – 'Hayseed fake! Always strumming his *geetar*. Everything about Sandburg is studied – except his poetry.'

From time to time the vatic voice took on a sound of Olympian melancholy, as a god might meditate upon the folly of humankind from above. 'Everything I've learned about life can be summed up in three words: "It goes on."'

(Yet even these somber reflections, the poet presented to the interviewer as one might hold out, in the palm of his hand, the most exquisite little gems.)

'And what *is* poetry, Mr Frost?'

'Poetry is – what is lost in translation.'

Mr Frost paused, then continued, thoughtfully: 'A poem is a stream of words that begins in delight and ends in wisdom. But, as it is poetry and not prose, it is a kind of music – a matter of sound in the ear. I hear everything I write.'

This I took up with a canny little query: 'Do you mean you *hear* – literally, Mr Frost? Words in your head?'

Mr Frost frowned. Though he liked very much to be listened to, he did not like being queried. 'I – speak aloud – to myself. The poem is a matter of measured syllables, iambics, for instance, that produce a work of – poetry.' Abruptly he ceased. What sense did this make? The young woman interviewer gazing at him so avidly with her widened heal-all-blue eyes had become just subtly disconcerting.

'A poem is "sound over sense"?'

'No. A poem is not "sound over sense" – not my poetry! The babbling of that pretentious prig Tom Eliot might qualify, or infantile lower-case e.e. cummings – but not the poetry of Robert Frost.'

And again cannily I asked, 'Do you ever "hear voices", Mr Frost? As you are composing your poems?'

Mr Frost frowned. The large jaws clenched. A look of something like fright came into the icy eyes. 'No. I did not – ever – "hear voices". The poet is not, as Socrates seemed to believe, in the grip of a "demon" – the poet is *in control* of the "demon".'

'But there is a "demon"?'

'No! There is not a "demon" – this is a way of speaking metaphorically. Poetry is the speech of metaphor.'

Mr Frost was frowning at me, dangerously; yet I persisted, with my innocently naïve questions: 'But, Mr Frost – what *is* metaphor? And why is metaphor the speech of poetry?'

The poet snorted with the sort of derision that would have roused gales of laughter in an admiring audience. 'Dear Miss Fife! You might as well ask a mocking bird why he sings as he does, appropriating the songs of other birds, as ask a poet why he speaks as he does. If you have to ask, my dear girl, it may be that you are incapable of understanding.'

This scathing rejoinder that would have eviscerated another, more subtle interviewer did not deter me, for I felt the truth of the poet's observation, and did not resent it.

'But you have never "heard voices" and you've never claimed to have "second sight"?' – I pressed these issues, for I knew that

Mr Frost would not volunteer any truth about himself that might detract from his image of the homespun New England bard.

'Miss Frost, I've told you – *no*.'

'And you've never had – "second sight"?'

Scornfully Mr Frost asked, 'What is "second sight"?'

'The ability to see into the future, Mr Frost. To feel premonitions – to prophesize.'

Mr Frost snorted in derision. In his eyes, a small flicker of alarm. 'Old wives' tales, my dear. Maybe in your Scots family, but not in mine.' Adding then, in a smaller voice, 'Why would anyone want to "see into the future"! That would be a – a – curse . . .'

In the elderly poet's face an expression of such pain, such loss, such grief, such terror of what cannot be spoken, I looked aside for a moment in embarrassment. Thinking *But he is just an old, lonely man. It is mercy he deserves, not justice.*

And for that moment thinking perhaps I would take pity on him, beginning by destroying the humiliating snapshots in my Kodak Hawkeye. Then Mr Frost resumed his bemused, chiding, superior masculine voice: 'Miss Fife! Tell your avid readers that poetry is very *mystery*. Quite above the heads of all. No matter what the poet tries to tell you.'

But readily I countered: 'Yet, the poet builds upon predecessors. Who have been your major influences, Mr Frost?'

Mr Frost looked at me startled, as if a child had reared up to confront him. 'My – "influences"? Very few . . . *Life* has been my influence.'

'But not Thomas Hardy?'

'No.'

'Not Keats, not Shelley, not Wordsworth, not William Collins—'

'No! Not to the degree that *life* has been my influence.'

The thundery look in Mr Frost's face warned me not to pursue this line of questioning, for of all sensitive issues it is 'influences' that most rankle and roil even the greatest geniuses, like the suggestion that others have helped them crucially in their careers. Yet I couldn't resist asking why Frost had so low an opinion of Ezra Pound, who'd been extremely generous to him when he'd been a struggling unpublished poet when they'd first met in England.

Mr Frost shut his eyes, shook his head vigorously. No comment!

'Was Ezra Pound mistaken, or some sort of "fake", when he said that *A Boy's Will* contained "the best poetry written in America in a long time"?'

Mr Frost's eyes remained shut. But his large, lined face sagged in an expression of regret.

'Well – even a, a "fake" – can be correct, now and then.' Cautiously Mr Frost opened one of the faded-blue eyes, his gaze fixed upon me in mock appeal. 'As a clock that can't keep time is yet correct twice each twenty-four hours.'

Still, I wasn't to be placated. My next question was a sharp little blade, to insert into the fatty flesh of the poet, between the ribs: 'But, Mr Frost, weren't you once a friend of Ezra Pound's?'

'Miss Fife, why are you tormenting me with Pound? The man is a traitor to poetry, as he was a traitor to his country. A Fascist fool, an ingrate. No one can estimate when he became insane – he's insane *now*. Enough of Pound!'

'And what is your opinion of Franklin Delano Roosevelt?'

This was a sly question. For Mr Frost's Yankee conservatism was well known. Even more than Ezra Pound, FDR enraged the poet who stammered in indignation: 'That – cripple! That Socialist fraud! FDR's brain was as deformed as his body! Tried to hide the fact that he wasn't a whole man – the idiot voters were taken in. And his wife – homely as the backside of a gorilla! Socialism is plain theft – taking from those of us who work, and work damned hard, and giving what we've earned to idlers and shirkers. My wife, Elinor, a sensitive, educated woman, nonetheless raved about FDR that if she could, she would've killed him! – which suggests the man's monstrousness, that he would provoke a genteel woman like Elinor Frost to such rage. You may call me selfish, Miss Fife – yes, I am a "selfish artist" for I believe that art must be self-generated, and has nothing to do with the collective. "Doing good" is a lot of hokum! I would not give a red cent to see the world "improved" – for, if it were,' and here Mr Frost's voice quavered coyly, for he'd made this remark numerous times to numerous interviewers, 'what in hell would we poets write about?'

My shocked response was expected, too. And my widened blue eyes.

'Why, Mr Frost! You can't mean that . . .'

'Can't I! I certainly do, dear Evangeline. Have you not read my poem "Provide, Provide" – in a nutshell, there is Frost's economic theory. Provide for yourself even if it means selling yourself – "boughten" friendship is better than none.' The chuckle came, deep and deadly. 'Just don't expect *me* to provide for *you*.'

'But – you are acquainted with poverty, Mr Frost, aren't you? Quite extreme poverty?'

'No.'

'N-no? Not when you were a child, and later when you were married and trying to support a young family on your grandfather's farm in Derry . . .'

'No! The Frosts were frugal, but we were not – ever – *poor*.'

'When your father died in San Francisco, your mother was not left – destitute?'

'Miss Fife, "destitute" is an extreme word. I think that you are insulting my family. This line of questioning has come to an end.'

Mr Frost's face was flushed with indignation, of the hue of an overripe tomato. He'd been striking the swing seat beside him with the fly swatter as if he'd have liked to be striking *me*.

'You don't think that we have a moral duty to take care of others? Did Wordsworth feel that way?'

'Wordsworth! What did Wordsworth *know*! The old windbag didn't have to contend with our infernal IRS tax, Miss Fife! He did not have to contend with the slimy New Deal!'

Between us there was an agitation of the air. The very lemonade in my glass quivered, as if the earth had shaken.

Seeing that the poet was about to banish me, having lost patience with even my wanly blond good-girl looks, I plunged boldly head-on: 'Is it true, Mr Frost, that as a young man not yet married you were so depressed you tried to commit suicide in the Dismal Swamp of North Carolina?'

Mr Frost's cheeks belled in indignation. '"Dismal Swamp"!

Who has been telling you such – slander? It is not true . . .'

'Didn't you suspect that Elinor had been unfaithful to you, and so you wanted to punish her, and yourself, in a romantic gesture?'

'Ridiculous! It's for effete poets like Hart Crane to commit suicide – or utter fakes or failures like Chatterton and Vachel Lindsay – not whole-minded poets. A man with a wife and a family to bind him to the earth doesn't go gallivanting off and *kill himself*.'

'But your poems are filled with images of darkness and destruction, Mr Frost. The woods that are " ███████████████ " – except the speaker has " ████████████████████████████ ██████████████ ". The poem is obviously about a yearning to die, but a resistance to that yearning, and a regret over the resistance.'

'Balderdash, Miss Fife! Though you are a pretty lass, you are also a hysterical female. Reading into poems nasty little messages that aren't there, like looking into a mirror and seeing a snake-headed female who *is there*, and who has your secret face.'

Vehemently the poet spoke, and not very coherently. The red flushed face swelled and throbbed as with an incipient stroke. Yet, I persisted: 'Why don't you ever read your "dark" poems to audiences, Mr Frost? Why only your perpetual favorites, which audiences memorized in school? Are you afraid that they will be offended by the darker, more difficult poems, and wouldn't applaud you as usual? Wouldn't give you standing ovations that so thrill your heart? Wouldn't buy your books in such great numbers?'

Flush-faced Mr Frost told me that I had no idea what I was saying. And that I'd better turn off the damned tape recorder, or he would smash it. 'Enough! This ridiculous interview is concluded. I suggest that you leave now – exactly the way you crept in.'

Yet boldly I asked Mr Frost about his patriotic poem of 1942 'The Gift Outright', with its remarkable line '██████████████ ██████████████████ ': 'Could you explain to the readers of *Poetry Parnassus* what this astonishing statement means?'

Mr Frost had taken up the dingy red plastic fly swatter, tapping it restlessly against the swing railing. His voice was heavy with sarcasm: 'Assuming the readers of *Poetry Parnassus* can comprehend English, I see no reason to "explain" a single word.'

'Mr Frost, this is indeed a provocative statement!'

'Damn you, Fife, what are you getting at? Frost is not "provocative" – Frost is "consoling". Audiences have loved "The Gift Outright" whether they understand it or not. The poem tells us that our ancestors, who settled the New World, were "of the land" in a way that later generations can't be, because we are American citizens; and that the "land" – our country, America – is a "gift outright". It is *ours*.'

Seeing the expression on my face, which was one of utter transparency, the poet said irritably, 'Is it each individual word that perplexes you, Miss Fife, or their collective meaning?'

'Mr Frost, the collective meaning of your poem seems to endorse "Manifest Destiny" – the right of American citizens to claim all of North America, virtually. It totally excludes native Americans – the numerous tribes of Indians – who lived in North America long before the European settlers arrived. British, Spanish invaders – "Caucasians".'

Mr Frost cast me a smile of glaring incredulity. 'Miss Fife! For God's sake – are you seriously suggesting that Indians are *native Americans?*'

'Yes! They are human beings, aren't they?'

'*Human*, but primitive. *Beings*, but closer to the animal rung of the ladder than to our own.' Mr Frost tapped the fly swatter on his knee, with a dangerous squint of his eye. 'You may put this in your interview, Miss Fife, that Robert Frost believes in *civilization* – which is to say the *Caucasian civilization*.'

'But, Mr Frost, the indigenous people you call "Indians" were the original *native Americans*. Caucasians from the British Isles and from Europe came to this continent as settlers, explorers and tradesmen – with no respect for the native Americans living here, they appropriated the land, exploited and attempted genocide against the natives, and are doing so even now, in less obvious ways, in many parts of the country. And your poem "The Gift Outright", which might have addressed this issue with a poet's sharp eye, instead—'

Smirking, Mr Frost interrupted, with a sharp slap of the fly swatter, 'Miss Fife! "Genocide" is a pretty highfalutin term for what our brave settlers did – conquered the wilderness, established a decent civilization . . .'

'But there was not a "wilderness" here – there were Indian civilizations, living on the land. Of course, the original inhabitants were not *city dwellers* – they lived in nature. But – surely they had their own civilizations, different from our own?'

How surprised Mr Frost was, by the passion with which I

spoke! Almost you might have thought, as Mr Frost was possibly thinking, that there was something *not quite right* about this interviewer from *Poetry Parnassus* with her tape recorder and notebook and straw satchel who was persisting, despite the poet's obvious agitation: 'Mr Frost – is it possible that your audiences have been deceived, and that you aren't a "homespun New England bard" but something very different? An emissary from "dark places" – an American poet who sees and defends the very worst in us, without apology – in fact, with a kind of pride?'

'And what is wrong with pride, Miss Fife!'

A fierce light shone in the poet's eyes. His breath came audibly and harshly. You could sense the old, enlarged heart beating in his chest like a maddened fist as in the throes of a combative sexual encounter at which the poet in his inviolable *maleness* did not intend to fail.

But the interviewer was suffused with a sort of ferocity, too. Squaring her slender shoulders, leaning forward so that her pale-blond hair fell softly about her face, daring to inquire in her throaty, thrilled voice that hardly seemed the voice of a young virginal woman: 'Did you not once say, Mr Frost, imagining that your remark wouldn't be recorded, that you'd have liked never to see your children again – those who were living at the time, and causing you so much trouble; they were – are – "accursed" –'

'I – I did not say that . . . Who has been spreading such lies? I – did not . . .'

'You've written about this – in your sly, coded poems. Your inability to feel another's pain – your inability to touch another person. You've revealed everything in your poems that has been hidden in your heart. Which is why, in public, you deny your very poems – as one might deny paternity to a deformed or disfigured child.'

'This is false – this is wrong! I have tried to explain...' Mr Frost drew a deep breath, shut his eyes tight and began to recite through clenched jaws: "'

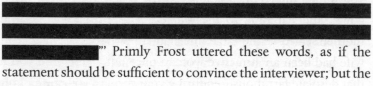

"' Primly Frost uttered these words, as if the statement should be sufficient to convince the interviewer; but the statement did not have the desired effect.

'Mr Frost, what do those words even mean? That those who see in your poetry something of the terribly flawed and dishonest man who wrote the poems are charged with being "ungraceful"? – while the poet, who feeds like a vampire upon the lives of others, is imagined as being "graceful"?'

'But – that's what poetry *is*.'

'Not all poetry! Not all poets. The subject today is *you*.'

'I – I – I have no reply to that, Miss...' The fly swatter had fallen from the poet's fingers onto the ground. His fingers appeared frozen, claw-like as if cramped. '... whoever you are, and wherever you are from – Hell...'

'But do you believe in "Hell", Mr Frost?'

'I – I think that I do ... I must ... I believe – "This is Hell, nor am I out of it." That grim and beautiful line of Marlow's, I do believe.'

This concession, rare for the poet, failed utterly to placate the interviewer, who pursued her panting quarry like a huntswoman and showed him no mercy.

'Mr Frost, do you remember when your daughter Lesley was six years old? When you were still a young man – a young father – living on that wretched farm in Derry, New Hampshire? You wakened your daughter with a loaded pistol in your hand and you forced the terrified child to come downstairs in her night-gown, and barefoot, to the kitchen, where the child saw her mother seated at the table, her hair in her face, weeping. Your wife had been an attractive woman once but, living with you in that desolate farmhouse, enduring your moods, your rages, your sloth, your fumbling incapacity as a farmer, your sexual bullying and clumsiness, already at the age of thirty-one she'd become a broken, defeated woman. You told the child Lesley that she must choose between her mother and her father – which of you was to live, and which to die. "By morning, only one of us will be alive."'

'No. That did not – happen . . . It did not.'

'Yet Lesley remembers it vividly, and will reproach you with the memory through your life, Mr Frost. Is she mistaken?'

'My daughter is – yes, mistaken . . . My eldest daughter hates me without knowing me. She has never understood me . . .'

'And what of your daughter Irma, committed to a mental hos-pital? Why did you give up on Irma, when you might have helped her more? Were you exasperated and disgusted by her, as an extreme form of yourself? Your wild talk, your turbulent moods, your "dark places"? You gave up on Irma as you'd given up on your sister Jean years before. Mental illness frightens you, like a contagion.'

Mr Frost protested, weakly: 'I did all that I could for Irma, and for – my sister Jean. I could not be expected to give up my entire life for them, could I? All that I'd done, they felt no gratitude for, but were encouraged in their wildness and blame of *me* . . .'

'Why was poor Irma so obsessed with being kidnapped and raped? Forced into prostitution? You were scornful of Irma's terrors, you'd told her bluntly when she was just a girl that she was so unattractive, she needn't fear being raped; no man would be interested in her sexually; she wasn't worth "twenty cents a throw". Later, to Robert Lowell, you said laughingly that Irma Frost couldn't have "made a whorehouse".'

'That is not true. That is – a lie, slander . . . Lowell was a sick, distressed person. I spoke to him in a way to lift his spirits, to entertain him. He'd thought that he was *bad*, but old Frost was *badder*. But none of it was meant to be taken literally . . .'

'And your son. Your only surviving son. He'd said, "My father is ashamed of me. My father has done no more than glance at my poetry, and push it aside." He'd said, "Sometimes I feel tight-strung – like a bow. I feel that I want to – that I must – be shot straight to the heart of . . ." And your son's voice would trail off, and he would hide his face in his hands.'

The interviewer spoke in a soft condemning voice. The poet stared at her, uncomprehending. Small hairs stirred at the nape of his neck. It was very hard for him to draw breath. Barely he managed to stammer, 'Who? Who is – "he"? Who are you speaking of . . .' A sensation of vertigo swept over him, the ground seemed to be opening at his feet. In desperation he'd snatched up the poetry notebook in both hands as if to shield himself with it.

'Mr Frost, you know that he burned his poetry. Fifteen years of poems. You'd thought so little of him, you'd never given him permission to live. He was always your "son" – you never relinquished him, though you never loved him. He was thirty-eight when he died of a gunshot wound to the head. He'd seemed much younger, as if he'd never lived. All he wanted was approval from you, a father's blessing – but you withheld it.'

'I've told you – I don't know what – who – you are talking about . . .'

'Your son, Mr Frost. Your son Carol, who killed himself.'

'My son did not – kill – himself . . . He died of a regrettable accident.'

'Your son you named with a ridiculous girl's name, for some whim of yours. He was so unhappy with "Carol" he changed it to "Carroll" – to your displeasure. It was too late, the damage had been done, as a young child he'd been marked. In his poetry he wrote of how you'd sucked the marrow out of his bones. You'd left him nothing, you'd taken his manhood from him. He knew your secret – you could never love any of your children, you could love only yourself.'

Frost shook his massive head from side to side, frowning. Deep rents in his ashy skin.

'I – I loved Carol. He knew . . .'

'You never told him you loved him! He didn't *know*.'

'Carol was weak – immature. He *was not* a man. How then could he write genuine poetry? He was a versifier – his best poems were pale imitations of mine. He was a child who has traced drawings in Crayola. His rhymes were stolen from mine – "though" – "snow" – "slow" – "near" – "seer". Worse were his poems in which he'd attempted *vers libre*.' Mr Frost laughed, a ghastly wheezing sound like choking. With the verve of a litigator arguing his case, the poet spoke with a righteous sort of confidence, though laced with regret: 'My son thought that "no one loved him". Pitiful! His mind was one cloud of suspicion . . . his cloud became our cloud. Well, he took his cloud away with him. We never gave him up. He ended it for us – the protracted misery and *obstinacy* of a failed life.' A brooding moment, and then: 'It was an error to marry – initiating a sequence of worse errors, the Frost children. Soon it came to me, though I thought I'd kept it a secret, that I didn't care in the slightest if I ever saw any of them again – at least, after my dear daughter Marjorie died. *She*, I did love. I loved very much. Yet, what good was my love? I could not save the beautiful girl. She died as the child of anyone might have died – a disappearance. "███████████████████████████████████ ███████████████████" – nothing more in nature than that, of grief. A poet ought not to marry, and procreate. That was the fear of my wife, Elinor – she would drag me down into her mortality, and we would make each other miserable, which we did. Poetry is more than enough of "procreation". Life is the raw material, like dough – but it is only "raw", and it is only "dough". No one cares to eat mere *dough*.'

The poet's large, slack-jowled face contorted into a look of sheer disdain, disgust. Astonishingly he reared up onto his legs, which barely held his bulk. The porch swing creaked in protest. The notebook fell from his lap, onto the grass. Like a wounded bull, suffused with an unexpected strength by pain and outrage, the poet swayed and glared at his tormentor. He was stricken to the heart, or to the gut – but he would not succumb. His enemies had assailed him cruelly and shamefully as they had through his beleaguered life but *he would not succumb.*

'You – whoever you purport to be – an "interviewer" for a third-rate poetry journal – what do you know of *me*? You may know scattered facts about my "life" – but you don't know *me*. You haven't the intelligence to comprehend my poems any more than a blind child could comprehend anything beyond the Braille she reads with her fingertips – only just the raised words and nothing of the profound and ineffable silence that surrounds the words.'

Taken by surprise, the young blond interviewer stumbled to her feet also, a deep flush in her face; in dampened undergarments and schoolgirl floral-pink 'shirtwaist' she gripped the straw bag, and backed away with a look of surprise and alarm.

Jabbing at this adversary with his forefinger, the enraged poet charged: 'You are *nothing*. People like you *don't exist*. You've never been called the "greatest American poet of the twentieth century" – you've never won a single Pulitzer Prize, let alone several Pulitzer Prizes – *and you never will*. You have never roused audiences to tears, to applause, to joy – you've never roused audiences to their feet in homage to your genius. Barely, you are qualified to *kiss the hem of genius*. Or – another part of the poet's anatomy. All you can do, people like you, contemptible little people, spiritual dwarfs, is to scavenge in the detritus of the poet's life without grasping the fact that the poet's *life* is of no consequence to the poet – essentially. You snatch at the dried and outgrown skin of the snake – the husk of a skin the living snake will cast off as he moves with lightning speed out of your grasp. You fail to realize that only the *poetry* counts – the *poetry* that will prevail long after the poet has passed on, and you and your ilk are gone and forgotten utterly, as if you'd never existed.'

The poet stumbled down the porch steps, not quite seeing where he was going. Something glaring was exploding softly – the sun? Blazing, blinding light? Overhead, an agitated *soughing* in the trees? He had banished her, the demon. His deep-creased face was contorted with rage. The faded-icy-blue eyes were sharpened like ice picks. In the grass, the poet's legs failed him, he began to fall, he could not break the propulsion of his fall, a fall that brought him heavily to the ground, the stunning hardness of the ground beneath the grass; all his life he'd been eluding the petty demons that picked at his ankles, his legs; the petty demons that whispered curses to him, that he was bad, he was wicked, he was cruel, he was *himself*; all his life they'd tried to elicit him to injure himself, as his only surviving son, Carol, had injured himself, and succumb to madness. In the vast reaches of the Dismal Swamp he'd first seen the demons clearly, and retained the vision through the decades; how, in daylight, it is a temptation to forget the terrible wisdom of the Swamp, and of the night; but at great peril. He had blundered this time, but he had escaped in time. *He was not going mad* – but madness swept through him like a powerful emetic.

Somehow, he was lying in the grass. Gnats flung themselves against his damp eyes. He'd fallen from a great height, like a toppled statue, too heavy to be righted. His fury was choking him. Like a towel stuffed down his throat. Somewhere close by a clock was ticking loudly, mockingly. He would grab hold of the damned clock and throw it – but the taunting girl-interviewer had vanished.

His notebook! Precious notebook! It had slipped from his fingers, he strained to reach it, to hold it against his chest. Strangely it seemed that he was bare-chested – so suddenly. The shame of his soft, slack torso, the udder-like breasts, was exposed to all the world. He could not call for help, the shame was too deep. The poet was not ever a weakling to call for help. The obstinacy of his aging flesh had been a source of great frustration to him, and shame, but he had not succumbed to it, and he would not.

Just barely, the poet managed to seize hold of a corner of the notebook. The strain of so reaching caused him to tremble, to quaver – yet, he managed to draw the notebook to him, and to press it against his chest. His loud-thumping heart would be protected from harm, from the assault of his enemies. For here was his shield, as in antiquity – the warrior has fallen, but is shielded from the pain of mortality.

'Mr Frost? Oh – Mr Frost—'

Already they'd found him, he'd had scarcely time to rest. He was unconscious, yet breathing. The great poet fallen in wild grass in front of the Poet's Cabin at Bread Loaf, Vermont, in a languorous late afternoon in August 1951.

Yet, the poet was breathing. No mistaking this, the poet was breathing.

This is a work of fiction, though based upon (limited, selected) historical research. See Robert Frost: A Biography by Jeffrey Meyer *(1996).*

COPYRIGHT

Autumn 2003; 'Cynthia Ozick interviews Henry James', *Zembla*, issue 2, Winter 2003; 'Geoff Dyer interviews Friedrich Nietzsche', *Zembla*, issue 5, Summer 2004; 'Rick Moody interviews Jimi Hendrix', *Zembla*, issue 6, Autumn 2004; 'Ian Rankin interviews Arthur Conan Doyle', *Zembla*, issue 7, Winter 2004; 'David Mitchell interviews Samuel Johnson', *Zembla*, issue 8, Summer 2005.